P9-CEA-788

the ¡salpicón! cookbook

the ¡salpicón! cookbook
contemporary mexican cuisine

by Priscila Satkoff with Vincent Satkoff

Foreword by Charlie Trotter

Photographs by Jeff Kauck

CHRONICLE BOOKS
SAN FRANCISCO

Page 191 constitutes a continuation of the copyright page.

Library of Congress Cataloging-in-Publication Data available.

ISBN: 978-0-8118-6046-8

Manufactured in the United States of America

Design by Jane Gittings
This book has been set in Univers Light Condensed, Cholla, and Los Feliz

10 9 8 7 6 5 4 3 2 1

Chronicle Books LLC
680 Second Street
San Francisco, California 94107

www.chroniclebooks.com

acknowledgments

A word of thanks to all those who made ¡Salpicón! and therefore this book, possible:

My mother and grandmother, who started me on my culinary journey;

My father, who taught me the difference between eating and dining;

My mother-in-law, Rose, for her love and support and for being the best friend a girl could have;

Charlie Trotter, for his inspiration, friendship, and support;

Slobodan (Mike) and Mira Pavlovic, our original landlords, who believed in us from the beginning and said, "You kids can do it; in America anything is possible if you work hard!"

Terri Bimm, my culinary assistant, for testing and retesting all the recipes in the book (all the while missing many a White Sox game);

All our loyal regulars who have supported ¡Salpicón! from the beginning;

Our wonderful staff, many of whom have been with us for more than 10 years, and in particular, my sous chef, German Benítez, who makes my job easier every day;

Rick Rodgers, for putting my words on paper;

The wonderful team at Chronicle Books (Catherine Huchting, Kevin Toyama, Pamela Geismar, Mikayla Butchart, Beth Weber, and Jane Gittings) for their guidance and patience with this project;

An extra big thanks to Jeff Kauck, for his artful and beautiful photos, perfectly styled by Jen Strauss;

And last, but certainly not least, to my husband Vincent, for asking me 22 years ago four of the most important questions of my life: 1. Do you like wine? (Yes.) 2. Do you like cheese? (Yes.) 3. Do you like garlic? (Yes.) and 4. Will you marry me? (Yes! Yes! Yes!) And soon after that, I began my restaurant career!

Priscila Satkoff

table of contents

foreword 11

introduction 13

on wine 17

ingredient glossary 21

entremeses appetizers 28

bacon-wrapped sea scallops **callos de hacha con tocino** 30

grilled cactus and seafood napoleons with chipotle cream **nopales rellenos con mariscos y chipotle** 33

langoustines with "raw" green salsa **langostinos con salsa verde cruda** 34

fish seviche **seviche de pescado clásico** 37

lobster seviche with oranges and serranos **seviche de langosta con naranjas y serranos** 38

grilled shrimp with two sauces **camarones al carbón con dos salsas** 41

crab cakes with avocado-habanero sauce **tortas de jaiba con salsa de aguacate y habanero** 43

tequila-cured salmon tartare with tuna **tártaro de salmón curado al tequila y atún** 47

"chopped" guacamole **guacamole picado** 48

stuffed jalapeños with chihuahua cheese **jalapeños rellenos de queso chihuahua** 51

grilled portobellos with chipotle sauce **portobellos enchipotlados a la parrilla** 52

stuffed poblano chiles with avocado and potatoes **poblanos rellenos con papas y aguacate** 55

squash blossoms stuffed with goat cheese **flores de calabaza con queso de cabra** 56

cold marinated beef brisket **salpicón de carne** 59

shredded pork with roasted tomatoes and chipotle chiles **tinga de puerco** 60

pork picadillo turnovers **empanadas de picadillo** 62

mixed-mushroom tacos **tacos con hongos** 64

black bean and chihuahua cheese tamales **tamales de frijoles negros con queso** 68

zucchini and chipotle tamales **tamales de calabaza y chipotle** 69

cheese and chile tamales **tamales de queso fresco y chile serrano** 70

soups and salads sopas y ensaladas 72

lentil soup **sopa de lentejas** 74

mexican-style gazpacho with spicy cucumber sorbet
  gazpacho mexicano con nieve de pepino y serrano 77

chilled avocado and crab soup **sopa fría de aguacate y jaiba** 78

corn soup with star anise **sopa de elote y anís** 81

grilled octopus salad **ensalada de pulpo** 82

purslane salad **ensalada de verdolagas** 85

spinach salad with chipotle-honey dressing **ensalada de espinaca con aderezo de chipotle y miel** 86

cactus salad **ensalada de nopales** 89

christmas eve salad **ensalada de nochebuena** 90

seafood entrées mariscos 92

halibut in parchment with tequila **pescado al tequila** 94

salmon with red papaya–tequila sauce **salmón con salsa de papaya roja y tequila** 97

ancho-glazed salmon with fennel **salmón al hinojo glaseado con chile ancho** 98

black sea bass with mushrooms and two sauces **pescado con hongos y dos salsas** 101

fish fillets veracruz-style **pescado a la veracruzana** 102

fish in caper sauce with stuffed chilaca chiles **pescado alcaparrado con chilacas rellenas** 105

soft-shell crabs with sweet garlic sauce **jaibas al mojo de ajo 106**

seafood stew **caldo de mariscos** 109

mussels with white wine, serranos, and cilantro
  mejillones al cilantro con vino blanco y chiles serranos 111

oysters in chipotle cream sauce **ostiones con crema de chipotle** 112

meat and poultry entrées carnes y aves 114

beef in green mole **carne en mole verde** 116

beef tenderloin filets with shiitakes in morita chile and tomatillo sauce
filetes de res con shiitakes en salsa de morita y tomatillo 119

veal chops with black bean and habanero sauce
chuleta de ternera en salsa de frijoles negros y habanero 120

pork chops with ancho-chile sauce **chuleta de puerco en salsa de chile ancho** 123

lamb shanks in oaxacan red mole sauce **mixiote de borrego en mole coloradito** 124

baby racks of lamb with a pumpkin-seed crust **costillitas de borrego con corteza de pepitas** 127

lamb loin chops in garlicky pasilla sauce **chuletas de borrego en salsa de pasilla** 128

chicken breasts in ginger mole **mole de jengibre con pechugas de pollo** 129

baby chickens with guajillo sauce **pollitos con salsa de guajillo** 130

duck two ways in ancho-almond sauce **pato almendrado** 133

duck leg confit with pomegranate **pierna de pato con granada** 135

grilled quail with ancho-honey sauce **codornices en salsa de chile ancho y miel** 139

side dishes guarniciones 140

roasted poblano strips with cream **rajas con crema** 142

potatoes with chorizo **papas con chorizo** 145

potatoes with spinach and onions **papas con espinaca y cebollas** 145

scalloped potatoes **papas con crema y queso añejo** 146

potato cakes with aged mexican cheese **tortas de papa con queso añejo** 146

pinto beans with chihuahua cheese and chiles **frijoles maneados** 149

pinto beans with bacon and poblano chiles **frijoles charros** 149

white rice **arroz blanco** 150

rice with poblano chiles **arroz a la poblana** 150

mexican rice **arroz mexicano** 153

spinach tamales **tamales de espinaca** 154

sauces salsas 156

árbol chile sauce **salsa de chile de árbol** 158

roasted tomato–chipotle sauce **salsa de jitomate asado y chipotle** 161

avocado-tomatillo sauce **salsa de aguacate y tomatillo** 162

"mortar" salsa **salsa de molcajete** 162

roasted tomatillo sauce **salsa de tomatillo asado** 165

ancho or guajillo chile purée **puré de chile ancho o guajillo** 165

ancho-honey sauce **salsa de chile ancho y miel** 166

four-chile sauce **salsa de cuatro chiles** 166

roasted poblano cream sauce **crema poblana** 169

cilantro oil **aceite de cilantro** 169

basic brine for meats **agua para marinar carnes** 170

mango sauce **salsa de mango** 171

desserts postres 172

warm chocolate-espresso cakes with coffee bean sauce
   pasteles de chocolate con crema de café 174

tequila truffles **trufas de tequila** 175

"three milks" cake **pastel tres leches** 176

rice pudding brûlée **arroz con leche caramelizado** 178

orange-flavored flan **flan de naranja** 179

pear and mango tartlets **tartaletas de pera y mango** 180

pineapple three ways **trío de piña** 183

prickly pear sorbet in lime tuiles **nieve de tuna con galletas de lima** 184

sources 187

index 188

table of equivalents 192

I have had the extraordinary pleasure and privilege of knowing Priscila and Vince Satkoff for more than 10 years. Further, I have had in excess of 50 meals (nay, *dining experiences*!) at their unbelievable restaurant, ¡Salpicón!

First, Priscila! She has emerged as not only one of Chicago's top chefs, but also as one of the very best chefs in America. Her insistence on using only the very best and most pristine ingredients already sets her apart. Beyond that, she brings something to her food that few chefs, however talented or trained, seem capable of providing to their completed dishes—namely an ability to infuse unabashed sensuality and unbridled passion onto the plate. I am so in awe and in love with her creations that when I invite the great European chefs to Chicago, I invariably take them to ¡Salpicón! for a taste of something special, and better still, something they would never see in their homelands. Priscila is, in every way, the high priestess of cooking modern, but authentic, Mexican cuisine! Love, passion, innovation, and purity literally infuse her food. Also, she pulls off a most difficult task—her food is ethereal and incredibly light, but simultaneously bursts with flavor.

Now, Vince! Vincent Satkoff is easily one of the best wine minds in all of Chicago. He runs an exceptional dining room service-wise and truly knows how to match great and esoteric wines and hard-to-find tequilas with Priscila's lovely and refined food. The one-two punch that Priscila and Vince bring to the table is nearly unmatched—anywhere!

In *The ¡Salpicón! Cookbook* you will find a selection of their classic dishes and some whimsical inspirations. All of the recipes are brilliant! This is food that will work for the home cook and the professional alike. The headnotes for each dish offer not just insights on the preparation and history of the cuisine, but better still, ideas on deviating from the plan! Vince's wine notes are equally invaluable. His poignant ideas on what to serve with each genius preparation are hugely insightful, while also inspiring interpretation.

I suppose had I only lived a block away from ¡Salpicón! I would not be writing these words. I fear I would be there so often that Priscila and Vincent would have long ago grown tired of me and would not have asked me to comment on their exciting and incredibly important book. Priscila and Vincent are the best!

Charlie

Charlie Trotter

introduction

salpicón 1: (Spanish) A splash or dash, similar to (Fr.) soupçon 2: (Sp.) A popular dish of shredded cooked beef, often served at room temperature 3: (Sp.) A spicy salsa from the Yucatán 4: (U.S. English) A fine restaurant in Chicago serving authentic contemporary Mexican cuisine in an upbeat and festive atmosphere.

¡Salpicón! has been a vibrant part of the lively Chicago restaurant scene for more than thirteen years, and along the way we have gathered some wonderful accolades. The multistarred restaurant reviews led to recognition, but we always had the appreciation of our customers, who came for the Mexican food that I love . . . and love to cook.

This cuisine is markedly different from the cooking that most Americans think of as Mexican food. When I first came to this country, I often did not recognize what was on the plates at so-called Mexican restaurants. I learned that this was really Tex-Mex food. I believed that if I could bring the authentic flavors of my country to Chicago, they would be embraced. I wanted to share the earthy *moles* made from seemingly disparate but actually harmonious ingredients, the piquant salsas, the wide variety of seafood dishes, the satisfying desserts. I knew that there was much more to Mexican cooking than burritos!

While ¡Salpicón!'s life started in 1995, I feel that I have always been in training to be a professional chef, even though I never received any formal education as one. (My degree is actually in art history, and I can assure you that the knowledge, or at least appreciation, of art is essential in cooking, where visual elements are so important.) When I was a little girl growing up in Mexico City, I loved vegetables—my mother had to coax me to eat meat. I was fascinated watching my mother and grandmother cook family meals. Our dinners took two distinct forms. My father worked for the railroads and often left on long trips. When he was

at home, dinner was large and sumptuous. As soon as he left, however, my mother and sisters and I returned to much simpler fare. But this showed me how good cooking can make others happy, even possibly seduce them.

One particular incident stands out. When I was around twelve, my mother and aunt were planning a family event, probably some cousin's birthday. I overheard, and begged to be allowed to make the rice for the party, which would include about thirty guests. I remember the look of exasperation on my mother's face, as she knew she had no choice but to teach her stubborn daughter how to make the dish.

That huge pot of rice was the beginning of my real journey to becoming a cook. It was a success, and complimenting the chef can be dangerous. I was hooked. I tried every new food that I came into contact with. I wrote down every recipe that appealed to me, collecting them in a large notebook. The recipes that my family taught me weren't enough, and I began experimenting with my own creations.

Soon I found myself in college, and during a vacation in Cozumel to soak up some sun, I met a wonderful American man named Vincent, who worked in the restaurant business in Chicago. Our friendship turned into a courtship. It wasn't long before Vincent proposed marriage. Well, actually, he didn't propose until he was sure that I liked red wine, garlic, and strong cheese, but once that was confirmed, we were married in Mexico City, and I packed my bags and moved with him to Chicago.

Vincent was a well-regarded sommelier and maître d' who had worked at some of Chicago's best restaurants, and he returned to this career. In order to keep the same hours as my husband, I decided to look for a restaurant job. My Mexican accent and basic English were not a hindrance when I got a job at Frontera Grill, Rick Bayless's wildly popular restaurant, which served the most authentic Mexican food I had come across since my arrival. I started out as a food dispatcher, bringing food to the tables, graduated to server, then ended up as Rick's personal assistant.

In the meantime, I was catering out of my apartment, making whatever was requested by my friends, preparing mountains of tamales and *albóndigas* (meatballs). When I left Frontera Grill, I wanted to start my own business, but for some reason, I didn't immediately see that a restaurant was the answer. I loved flowers—why not become a florist? I loved shoes almost as much as flowers—maybe a shoe store? Finally, probably when tasting a spoonful of my mole sauce, it hit me—I would open a great Mexican restaurant, starting with and branching out from my family recipes.

For the next two years, I threw myself into the creation of my restaurant. Vincent and I found a building on North Wells Street in a neighborhood that was not known as a restaurant area but did have many loft buildings housing artists and others, as well as huge apartment complexes with lots of hungry people. I considered every aspect of the design, from the bright hues I knew had to be a part of the color scheme, to the kind of exciting artwork

that would hang on the walls. The food would be based on what I knew from my years of cooking in Mexico and America, but it would contain the finest aspects of both. The ingredients would be the best, and the presentation would be inspired by the beautiful plates I saw at the terrific restaurants where Vincent had worked and I had dined.

As for the name, I wanted something both Mexican and gustatory. A shredded meat "salad," *salpicón* was not only one of my favorite dishes, but it also had the right "sound." I added Spanish exclamation points for emphasis, so the official name of my place would be ¡Salpicón!

We opened on a cold, snowy evening in January 1995. There was one customer in the restaurant that night—not a very auspicious beginning. But the truth is, because of my lack of experience behind the stove in a restaurant kitchen, I wonder if I could have handled a full house. I made every single thing on the menu by myself without any helpers. That involved a lot of roasting and peeling of chiles! As the guests came, I learned how to delegate, but it didn't happen overnight. But when you are young and haven't had a lot of life experience, you don't know the difference.

Since ¡Salpicón!'s birth, the American food scene has changed enormously. The inspiration for my cooking has always been the ingredients at hand. In Mexico, that meant everything from dark *huitlacoche* (a fungus that grows on corn) to electric-colored squash blossoms to an entire rainbow of chiles and peppers. I would enjoy dishes at other restaurants that are not necessarily part of my culinary heritage (for example, rack of lamb), and then think about how I could make them Mexican. When I came to Chicago, the Mexican community in the Pilsen neighborhood was well established, and there was no shortage of Latino grocery stores. Regardless, my creativity was somewhat restricted by what was available.

Slowly but surely, my purveyors started offering my favorite foods. There was the New Year's Eve when I wanted to serve the Mexican delicacy squash blossom soup—the bright gold petals are so celebratory and their flavor is unique. It took some doing, but the flowers were delivered, and our customers had a very special soup to ring in the New Year. Now, all over America, you can find *queso fresco* and other Mexican cheeses, just about every chile I ever had at my disposal back home, special corn flour for tamales, and more. In season, you are likely to find those squash blossoms at your local farmers' market. What you can't get at a large supermarket, you can order online.

But, almost more important, there is that great array of American products that make my cooking such a pleasure. Diver or day-boat scallops, Maine lobsters, tender and flavorful beef—I didn't have these to make meals with in Mexico. It is this marriage of fine fresh ingredients with ancient Mexican seasonings that makes ¡Salpicón!'s cuisine unique.

One very important aspect of ¡Salpicón!'s success is our commitment to serving excellent wines with our food. Like the people who erroneously think that Mexican food is tortilla chips with cheese sauce, there are those who believe they can only drink beer or a margarita with their enchiladas. Both Vincent and I know that outstanding food deserves equally fine wine. At first, some wine-lovers balked at the problem of matching wines with chiles and other bold spices. It was not a problem—perhaps a bit of challenge, but never an unpleasant issue to resolve. But just as the food purveyors began to offer more ingredients that inspired my cuisine, wines from all over the world became available for Vincent to offer to our guests, and more possibilities for happy matches presented themselves. Our wine list is extensive and one of the best in Chicago, if Vincent and I do say so ourselves. We also offer a huge selection of tequilas for sipping before and after the meal. And we will make you a darned good margarita if you ask.

With *The ¡Salpicón! Cookbook*, you can bring the zesty cooking of our restaurant into your own home. I share with you my passion for my country's cooking, but with a contemporary attitude that makes it more than just a collection of my family recipes. And with Vincent's wine notes, you can enhance the dining experience with a glass of great wine, just as if you had a sommelier by your side.

¡Buen provecho!

Priscila Satkoff
August 2008

Contrary to popular belief, wine is a great accompaniment to Mexican food. If you go to the typical Mexican restaurant, almost everyone has a margarita in front of them. A margarita may be a great beginning to a fine dinner (just as a martini or Manhattan), but with its strong alcoholic flavor, tart lime juice, and sweet orange liqueur, it is not convivial to food. After you have had your margarita cocktail, it is better to move on to a delicious wine.

Mexican cuisine is one of the most complex and oldest of all cuisines. The indigenous cultures drank fermented agave juice (pulque) and cacao beans ground up with many different ingredients (don't ask about the additions—let's just say it is hardly the hot cocoa we drink today). It wasn't until the Spanish conquistadors established themselves and their culture, however, that wine became important. Not all of Mexico's terrain is friendly to wine growing, so it didn't establish itself as a country with a wine-making tradition. (There is a burgeoning wine industry in some microclimates, and their wines are slowly showing up on wine-lovers' radars.) The fact that the wines that I like to serve with Mexican food are not Mexican is totally unimportant. As shown by countless centuries of tradition in the rest of Western civilization, wine and food are meant to be served together. And good food asks for (I would say that it demands) good wine.

I have made wine suggestions for almost all of the appetizers, main courses, and desserts in this book. These suggestions are not set in stone—many a happy pairing of wine and food was found through experimentation, and not as a rule in a book. You know your own personal likes and dislikes. But here are a few general tips to help you make good choices when putting together Mexican cuisine and wine.

White Wines

Heavily oaked white wines are to be avoided at all costs. Crisp, high-acid wines are extremely complementary to Mexican cuisine. Some winners include Austrian Grüner Veltliners and Rieslings from Austria, Alsace, Germany, or Australia; Pinot Gris from Oregon or Alsace; Alsatian Gewürztraminers; elegant French white Burgundies; unoaked Chardonnays, especially those from Oregon; and Sauvignon Blancs from many regions, including those of California, New Zealand, and the Loire Valley.

Red Wines

These can be a bit more of a challenge to pair correctly. While you should avoid heavily oaked wines, you do need to consider the tannin levels. Tannin and chiles are like brothers and sisters—they love to fight! Many people say that high alcohol levels of 14.0% or more acerbate the chile levels. I have found that if the wine has enough forward fruit, then the alcohol really does not interfere. If the wine is light on the fruit and heavy on the alcohol, however, the wine is not balanced and will kick up the chiles and make the dish taste much spicier.

Great reds to try start with Pinot Noir from cool growing regions like Oregon, New Zealand, or specific areas in California such as the Sonoma Coast, Santa Lucia Highlands, Santa Maria Valley, and Mendocino. California Zinfandels come in many styles, but watch out for the alcohol content— some of the bigger ones will fight with those chiles. The great wines of Spain, especially from Priorat, Montsant, and Ribero del Duero (in particular Vega Sicilia) are very good bets. The southern Rhône has three relatively easy to find wines that you can trust with Mexican food—Gigondas, Vacqueyras, and Châteauneuf-du-Pape. Look for the great Super Tuscans that have some age in the bottle, such as Ornellaia, Sassicaia, Guado al Tasso, Il Borro, and Tignanello. You can also rely on the wines of Piedmont, including Barbaresco, Barbera, Dolcetto, and last but not least, Barolo. From Southern Italy, Montevetrano is produced by the affable Silvio Imparato. My Sicilian favorites are Donnafugata or Planeta. When on a budget, the reds from Chile and Argentina are the ones to consider. Australian reds tend to be super-juicy and work very well with spice. Look for Shiraz, Grenache, and Cabernet Sauvignon. Sometimes, all three are blended together, which is no surprise, because the Aussies love to blend.

Wine and Sauces

When thinking of a wine to pair with a dish, think first about the sauce and the preparation rather than the actual protein. For example, Ancho-Glazed Salmon with Fennel (see page 98) would be great paired with an earthy Oregon Pinot Noir. Salmon with Red Papaya–Tequila Sauce (see page 97) would be better suited with a slightly fruity Viognier from California.

Wine and Chiles

In general, fresh chiles such as jalapeños, serranos, poblanos, *chiles de árbol fresco*, and habaneros tend to be best paired with white wines, while dried chiles such as anchos, guajillos, pasillas, chipotles, *moritas*, and *chiles de árbol seco* are best accompanied by reds.

¡Salud!

Vincent Satkoff
August 2008

principal ingredient

Fresh green chiles, such as jalapeños, poblanos, and serranos, found in such recipes as Langoustines with "Raw" Green Salsa (page 34).

Roasted tomatillos, found in the Lamb Loin Chops in Garlicky Pasilla Sauce (page 128).

Roasted Tomatillo Sauce, as served with Ancho-Glazed Salmon with Fennel (page 98).

Roasted Poblano Cream Sauce, as found in Squash Blossoms Stuffed with Goat Cheese (page 56).

Dried chiles, such as anchos and pasillas, as found in Lamb Shanks in Oaxacan Red Mole Sauce (page 124) and Pork Chops with Ancho-Chile Sauce (page 123).

Dried guajillo chiles in such dishes as Seafood Stew (page 109) and Baby Chickens with Guajillo Sauce (page 130).

Dried chipotle and morita chiles, such as those found in Grilled Portobellos with Chipotle Sauce (page 52) and Beef Tenderloin Filets with Shiitakes in Morita Chile and Tomatillo Sauce (page 119).

Habaneros are usually found only in their fresh state, as in Crab Cakes with Avocado-Habanero Sauce (page 43).

Fresh fruit salsas such as Mango Sauce (page 171) and Red Papaya–Tequila Sauce (page 97).

wines to pair	why they work
Sancerres and Pouilly-Fumés from France (Jolivet, Lucien Crochet), Sauvignon Blancs from California (Mason, Frog's Leap) and New Zealand (Villa Maria, Brancott); Rieslings from Germany (Balthazar Ress, von Buhl); and Grüner Veltliners from Austria (Prager, Hirsch).	These wines complement the herbaceous and fruity notes in the chiles and tame the medium-spicy heat.
German Rieslings (Carl Schmitt-Wagner, Robert Weil); Austrian Grüner Veltliners (Loimer, Hirtzberger) and Rieslings (Nigl, Hirsch); Rieslings from Alsace (Zind-Humbrecht, Trimbach) and Australia (Henschke, Penfolds). For reds, Italian Sangiovese (Antinori, Badia a Coltibuono) pairs well.	These high-acid wines stand up well to the sharp acidity in the tomatillos.
Big California Chardonnays (Kistler, Beringer); French white Burgundies (Domaine Leroy, Bourgogne Blanc); New World Pinots from California (Acacia, Rochioli) and Oregon (Domaine Serene, Ken Wright).	These wines will bring out the earthiness of the tomatillo while taming its acidity and will complement the richness of the cream.
Sancerres and Pouilly-Fumés from France (Domaine Fouassier, Lucien Crochet); Sauvignon Blancs from California (Geyser Peak, Duckhorn) and New Zealand (Cloudy Bay). For reds, look for New World Pinot Noirs from California (Sanford, Saintsbury), Oregon (Sokol Blosser, WillaKenzie), and New Zealand (Martinborough, Framingham).	Sauvignon Blancs by nature have an herbaceous quality, so they complement the vegetal component in the poblano. Earthy Pinot Noirs also pair well with the charred poblano.
For whites, look for French white Burgundies, particularly Meursaults (Vincent Girardin) and Puligny-Montrachets (Sylvain Langoureau Chassagne). For reds, consider Italian Nebbiolos (Barbarescos, not Barolos, such as Vietti and Bruno Giacosa) and French Syrahs from the northern Rhône (Côte-Rôtie Guigal, Jaboulet Cornas).	Earthy, mineral-scented white Burgundies match the earthy, coffeelike flavor of these dried chiles, which are primarily used in dark moles. Reds will work well as long as the tannin levels are low.
The same wines that pair with anchos and pasillas (see above).	The whites of Alsace have a beautiful fruit essence and a smoky quality that bring out the smokiness and spiciness of these chiles, and their high acidity tames the high heat. Fruit-forward Shirazes from Australia and California Zinfandels also have the guts to stand up to the intense heat and smoke.
Rieslings (Weinbach), Pinot Grises (Marcel Deiss), and Gewürztraminers (Hugel) from Alsace do well with these chiles. For reds, Australian Shirazes (d'Arenberg, Rosemount) and California Zinfandels (Cosentino, Burgess) fit the bill.	The same as above.
German Rieslings (Dr. Loosen); Austrian Grüner Veltliners (Loimer, Hirtzberger) and Rieslings (Allram, Nigl); Rieslings (Hugel, Trimbach), Gewürztraminers (Josmeyer), and Pinot Gris (Léon Beyer) from Alsace; and Rieslings from Australia (Grosset, Pikes).	These high-acid wines stand up well to the extraordinary heat level of the habanero (one of the hottest chiles in existence), while complementing the herbaceousness of the chile.
Full-bodied California Viogniers (Calera, Alban) and Chardonnays (Cakebread, Au Bon Climat); Australian tropical-style Chardonnays (Coldstream Hills); Alsatian Pinot Gris (Weinbach) and Muscats (Bott-Geyl). For red, a fruity California Pinot Noir (Buena Vista).	These wines bring out the tropical notes of the mango and papaya.

Of course, the best place to find Mexican ingredients for these recipes is a Latino grocery store. In places with a large Mexican population, such as California, Arizona, and Texas, you will discover many of these groceries at the supermarket. A quick search online will also uncover many sources (see page 187).

AVOCADOS: Look for the black-green Hass variety with the pebbly skin. The large, shiny green Caribbean avocados are bland and watery. It is difficult to find ripe avocados (they should yield when pressed with your fingers) at the grocer's, so buy them a few days before you want to serve them. Store the avocados in a closed brown paper bag to ripen at room temperature.

BEANS, DRIED: I cook beans day in and day out, so I speak with authority on the subject. They are a staple of Mexican cooking, so it is important to know how to cook them properly.

Buy your dried beans at a store that has a good turnover. Old beans are too hard and are difficult to cook to tenderness. Before cooking, remove any stones or shriveled beans, and rinse the beans in a colander.

To soak or not to soak? Some cooks insist on soaking the beans in cold water for a few hours or overnight (or by bringing them to a boil in water to cover, then letting the beans stand in the hot water for one hour) before draining and cooking in fresh water. They believe that soaking removes some of the enzymes in the beans that can make them difficult to digest. I do not find that soaking makes any difference in any way, and I think that it is a waste of time. If you are in the habit of soaking and draining dried beans, feel free to continue to do so.

It was once believed that salt toughens dried beans, lengthening the cooking time. This has been disproved, but there is another reason for adding salt at the end of the cooking time. Remember that the water will evaporate during cooking, and you could end up with oversalted beans. Let the beans cook until they are almost done, and then add the salt.

Although you may hear a lot about beans cooking best in clay pots, these pots are difficult to care for and may be covered with lead-based glaze, so they aren't worth the trouble. Just use a heavy-bottomed pot, keep the flame low so the beans cook at a nice, steady simmer, and you'll be in business. You shouldn't have to add more water, but if you do (which means either that your heat is too high or the pot is too wide), add boiling water from a kettle, not cold tap water, to keep the simmer constant.

CHEESE: Mexican-American cooks used to have to find substitutes for their favorite cooking cheeses. This is no longer true, as Mexican-style cheeses are easy to find in areas with Latino communities.

Queso Fresco: This is a soft, crumbly cheese, usually made from a mixture of cow and goat milk. The name means "fresh cheese," and it has a slightly acidic tang. It is often used as a garnish. Young, moist feta cheese is an acceptable substitute.

Queso Añejo: Literally, "aged cheese," this is queso fresco that has been allowed to age and harden enough to grate or break into firm crumbles. Use romano cheese if you can't find *queso añejo*.

Queso Chihuahua: This pale yellow, semisoft cheese comes from the Mennonite communities in northern Mexico. It is a popular melting cheese. Use Monterey Jack or a mild Cheddar if necessary.

CHILES: These spicy, savory fruits are probably the most essential flavor in Mexican cuisine. They are not always fiery hot, and you might be able to discern nuances of sweetness, vegetables, berries, wine, and other flavors in different chiles. (I insist on spelling "chiles" in the Mexican manner. "Chili" is a spicy Texan dish, and when capitalized, "Chile" is a country in South America.)

Chiles are mostly available fresh and dried. But a few chiles are canned or ground into pure chile powder (or mixed with other spices to create chili powder, a seasoning specific to that Texan dish). Most fresh chiles have a different name after they have been dried; for example, smoked jalapeños become chipotles, and poblanos become anchos.

Take care when handling chiles, as it is easy to transfer their volatile oils to the more tender parts of your body, especially your eyes. It's best to wear rubber gloves.

A lot of a chile's heat is concentrated in the seeds and veins. To control the heat of the dish, remove the veins and seeds, but set them aside. For more heat, simply add some of the seeds and veins. In many cases, I don't bother to remove the seeds and veins because I want the added heat.

Chiles are often given a number on the Scoville scale, named for the scientist who developed the method of gauging a chile's spiciness. Frankly, this indication is not very useful to the home cook—you will learn which chiles are the hottest by experience, and you won't find the Scoville number on any labels.

Here is a list of the chiles used in this book and some techniques used to cook with them:

Fresh Chiles

Fresh chiles are sometimes roasted to remove the tough skin and tenderize the flesh. While they can be roasted in an oven or over an open flame, it is easiest to broil them.

Roasting Fresh Chiles: Position a broiler rack about 6 inches from the heat source and preheat the broiler. Spread the chiles on a broiler pan. Broil the chiles, turning them occasionally with tongs, until they are blackened and blistered on all sides and the skin begins to separate from the flesh—do not burn a hole through the chiles. The broiling time will vary with the size of the chiles, but the average is about 10 minutes. Transfer the chiles to a plate and let cool to the touch. (Some people put the chiles in a bag to steam while they cool, but that lengthens the cooling time and could overcook the chiles.) Peel off the blistered skin and remove the stems, seeds, and veins.

Chilaca: About 10 inches long, this thin, green fresh chile is called a pasilla or *chile negro* when dried. Moderately hot, they are great roasted and stuffed.

Jalapeño: I use this familiar dark green chile often because it is readily available, but it isn't the only chile on the planet. The average jalapeño is tapered and 2 to 3 inches long. The red ones are ripened, and slightly sweeter. Crazed veins on the skin are not a sign of spoilage—use them anyway. As of late, jalapeños are much larger than in years past, and you can't always be sure of their heat level, so you may want to add them to your cooking with caution. It is interesting to note that they are named for the city of Xalapa near Veracruz, but they are no longer grown commercially there.

Poblano: Dark green and somewhat heart-shaped, this meaty chile is sometimes mistakenly called an ancho. It is only when dried that the poblano truly becomes an ancho chile. In California it is often incorrectly labeled as a pasilla.

Serrano: This looks like a smaller, thinner jalapeño, and has a similar flavor profile. The name means "from the mountains" in Spanish, and it was originally grown near Puebla. It is available in both green and red.

Dried Chiles

Drying chiles evaporates their juices, concentrating their flavor and giving them a leathery texture. The chile is usually soaked in hot water to soften it and puréed to create a smooth red sauce.

Soaking Dried Chiles: First, cut the chile lengthwise. Open the chile and remove any seeds and thin veins clinging to the interior. Discard the tough stem. Rinse the chiles under cold running water, just in case they have any dirt or grit clinging to the surface. Place in a small bowl and add boiling water to cover. Let them stand until softened, usually about 20 minutes. Drain in a sieve, reserving the soaking liquid. If the chiles are puréed in a blender or food processor, a little of the reserved liquid can be added to help the process along.

Toasting Dried Chiles: Dried chiles can be toasted before soaking to bring out their flavor, but it isn't essential. If a chile purée is going to be cooked in the recipe, I usually skip this step. To toast chiles, heat a dry, large, heavy skillet over medium-hot heat. Put the chiles in the skillet and cook, turning them occasionally, until the skin begins to change color in spots and you can smell the toasty aroma. The time varies according to the shape of the chile, but don't overtoast them or they will taste bitter. Remove the stems before using.

Ancho: This brick red, dried poblano has a relatively mild, sweet flavor. It is sometimes incorrectly labeled as a pasilla. The ancho is broad, while the pasilla is narrow.

Chile de árbol: This red "tree chile" is pencil thin and about 2 inches long. It is also available fresh by the same name.

Chipotle: This rust-colored, wrinkled chile is a smoked-dried jalapeño. Almost 20% of the jalapeño crop is turned into chipotles. You may occasionally see them labeled as *chiles ahumados*. They are available either simply dried or packed in a chile purée called *adobo* sauce.

Guajillo: Shiny and relatively flat, this deep orange-red chile has berrylike undertones. Because the skin is thicker than that of most dried chiles, it takes a bit longer to soak to tenderness.

Morita: Also smoked, this shiny black chile is similar to a chipotle, but is actually a smoked serrano.

Pasilla: A dried *chilaca* chile, this may also be called a chile negro. Pasilla means "little raisin," but this chile is long and black and, aside from its wrinkles, not very raisinlike.

Pequín: This small red chile is on the hot side. Most chiles get dark brown to black when dried, but like chiles de árbol, these are an exception.

Ground Chile

When buying ground chile, be sure it consists of pure powdered chiles and does not have any "filler" spices like cumin or oregano. Ground ancho and *pequín* chile is convenient to use in place of the whole chiles, which must be soaked first.

Canned and Bottled Chiles

The only canned chiles that I use are chipotles in adobo sauce. Adobo is a thick chile purée that clings to the chiles and is usually used in the recipe. When handling these fire bombs, be sure to wear rubber gloves. Leftover chiles and their sauce should be scooped into a small container, covered, and refrigerated, where they will keep for a week or so. For longer storage, individually freeze the chiles and any clinging adobo sauce on waxed paper. When hard, peel the chiles off the paper, transfer to a self-sealing plastic bag, and freeze for up to 2 months. You can purchase pickled jalapeños in bottles or cans at most supermarkets.

CILANTRO: This once exotic, now ubiquitous, herb needs little introduction, but there are tips on how to use it. Cilantro wilts quickly, so when you get it home from the market, stand the stems in a glass of water, tent with a plastic bag, and refrigerate. This will extend its shelf life by a couple of days.

To chop cilantro, remove the leaves from the stems. Rinse them well in a bowl of cold water to remove any sand or grit, then spin them in a salad spinner to dry completely. Dry cilantro is much easier to chop than wet.

CHORIZO, MEXICAN: This is a soft, fresh, bulk pork sausage that has been seasoned with ground chile—don't confuse it with Spanish chorizo, which is, by contrast, a smoked hard sausage. If you can't find Mexican chorizo, use 1 pound ground pork seasoned with 2 tablespoons American-style chili powder, 1 teaspoon salt, and 1 teaspoon red wine vinegar.

CREMA: This thick unpasteurized cream is not sour cream—the latter is much tangier. If you can't find it in the refrigerated section of a Latino supermarket, use crème fraîche, which you will find at specialty grocery stores.

JÍCAMA: Looking somewhat like a huge, squat potato, this vegetable is popular for its crisp texture.

NOPALES: Usually labeled by their Mexican name, these look just like what they are: cactus leaves. When cooked, they have a nice vegetal flavor, with a slightly slick texture similar to okra. The ones you buy at the market have usually had their thorns removed. If there are any recalcitrant ones, wear gloves to protect your hands, and pull the thorns out with pliers. Rinse the nopales well, but there is no need to peel them. There are also canned nopales, but I don't recommend them.

PILONCILLO: Cones of very hard brown sugar, these are easiest to measure if you crush them first with a mallet. While their flavor is richer than that of brown sugar, you can substitute the latter if you wish.

PRICKLY PEARS: The fruit of the same cactus that provides nopales, these deep red- or magenta-colored ovals make great desserts. Just pare them with a knife (the skin is too thick for a peeler) before using. They are usually puréed and strained to remove any tough seeds.

SEEDS AND NUTS:

Pine Nuts: In Mexico, the edible seeds from pine cones are called piñones. For the best price, buy them in bulk at Latino or natural-foods markets. Toast them first to bring out their buttery flavor (see Toasting Seeds and Nuts, page 26).

Pumpkin Seeds: Often called *pepitas,* these green, shelled seeds add flavor and texture to raw and cooked salsas (see Toasting seeds and Nuts, below).

Sesame Seeds: These are often used in moles. Buy them in bulk at Latino or Asian markets to get the best price.

Toasting Seeds and Nuts: Heat an empty skillet over medium heat. Add the sesame or pumpkin seeds or pine nuts and cook, stirring often, until they are very lightly browned and smell toasted. Keep the skillet lid handy to cover the pan if they start to jump out of the pan! Transfer them to a plate to cool—if you forget and leave them in the pan, they will surely burn.

TOMATILLOS: With their papery husks and tangy flavor, tomatillos are closely related to gooseberries, even though their name suggests kinship to tomatoes. Peel off the husk and rinse the tomatillos to remove their sticky natural coating before using.

TOMATOES, PLUM (ROMA): Like so many vegetables and fruits, these are worth using only when ripe and flavorful. They will always be at their best in the summer, but very good tomatoes from Florida are shipped all over the country throughout the year. The secret is to let them ripen at room temperature for a few days if they need it. Never refrigerate tomatoes, as the cold changes their texture and makes them mealy.

Roasting Tomatoes: Roasting tomatoes intensifies their sweetness. As with roasting chiles, this is easiest to do in the broiler. (You may also use a charcoal or gas grill, placing the tomatoes directly on the grill grids.) To roast tomatoes, position a broiler rack 6 inches from the source of heat and preheat the broiler. Leave the tomatoes intact—do not remove the stem end. Spread them on a broiler pan. Broil the tomatoes, turning them occasionally, until the skins are singed and splitting, about 5 minutes. The skins may get blackened, but do not overcook them, or the tomatoes will burst. Using tongs, carefully transfer the tomatoes to a platter (don't squeeze them!) and let cool. Remove the blackened skins. Remove the tough core end with the tip of a knife.

If a recipe calls for chopped roasted tomatoes, place a wire sieve over a bowl. Cut a peeled tomato in half horizontally. Use a forefinger to gently poke out as many seeds as you can without squashing the tomato, letting the seeds and juice fall into the sieve. Transfer the tomatoes to a food processor fitted with the metal chopping blade, add the strained juices to the bowl, and pulse a few times until the tomatoes are coarsely chopped. Do not try to chop the roasted tomatoes on a cutting board, as the juices will run all over.

Peeling and Seeding Tomatoes: You may want to remove the tough tomato skin and seeds from raw tomatoes. I don't do this too often, because I usually strain the tomato sauce. To peel tomatoes, bring a large saucepan of water to a boil. Add the tomatoes and cook until the tomato skin loosens, about 30 seconds. Using a slotted spoon, transfer the tomatoes to a bowl of ice water and let stand for a few minutes to cool, then drain and peel.

To seed tomatoes, cut the tomatoes in half crosswise through their "equators." Using a fingertip, poke the clusters of seeds in the tomato flesh to loosen them, and shake the tomato halves upside down over the sink.

entremeses
appetizers

callos de hacha con tocino
bacon-wrapped sea scallops

Sweet scallops and smoky bacon are excellent partners, as shown in this fine first course. The two components are joined with a bean purée that has been enlivened with intensely smoky morita chiles. Be sure to use only large sea scallops of the highest quality for this dish. Look for dry-packed scallops, which have not been treated with preservatives, unlike the common supermarket variety, which release a not-so-tasty liquid when cooked. **MAKES 4 SERVINGS**

MORITA BEAN PURÉE

1 cup dried navy beans, rinsed and picked over

½ teaspoon fine sea salt, plus more to taste

3 morita or dried chipotle chiles, seeded and deveined

3 cups boiling water

4 bacon slices

4 jumbo dry-packed (day-boat or diver) scallops

CRISPY LEEK

1 large leek, white and pale green parts only

Canola oil for deep-frying

2 tablespoons all-purpose flour

Fine sea salt and freshly ground black pepper

½ cup olive oil

Fine sea salt

2 tablespoons Cilantro Oil (page 169)

1. To make the purée: Bring 8 cups water to a boil in a large saucepan over high heat. Add the beans and reduce the heat to medium-low. Simmer until the beans are almost tender, about 1 hour. Add the ½ teaspoon salt and simmer until the beans are tender, about 30 minutes more. Drain the beans, reserving about 1 cup of the cooking liquid.

2. Put the chiles in a small bowl, cover with the boiling water, and let stand until softened, about 10 minutes. Process the beans and soaked chiles in a blender or food processor, adding a bit of the reserved bean cooking liquid as needed to make a coarse purée. Season with salt to taste. (The bean purée can be cooled, covered, and refrigerated up to 1 day ahead. If making ahead, cover and refrigerate the reserved cooking liquid as well. Reheat the purée over low heat, adding cooking liquid as needed to return the purée to a runny consistency.)

3. Cook the bacon in a large skillet over medium heat until half-cooked, about 3 minutes. Transfer to a plate and let cool. Trimming the bacon as needed, wrap 1 slice around the side of each scallop without overlapping the bacon, securing the bacon with a wooden toothpick. (The scallops can be covered and refrigerated up to 8 hours ahead.)

4. To prepare the leek: Cut leek lengthwise very thin and crosswise into 3- to 4-inch strips. Place the leek in a bowl of cold water and wash well to remove any dirt or grit. Lift the leek out of the water, leaving any grit, transfer to paper towels, and pat completely dry.

5. Pour canola oil into a heavy medium saucepan to a depth of 2 inches. Heat over high heat to 350°F (use a candy thermometer to check temperature). Place the leek in a bowl and toss with the flour and salt and pepper to taste. In batches, deep-fry the leek until golden brown and crisp, about 30 seconds. Using a wire-mesh skimmer, transfer to paper towels to drain. (The leek can be stored at room temperature for up to 2 hours.)

6. To serve, heat the beans in a saucepan over medium heat, stirring often, until hot. Set aside and keep warm. Heat the olive oil in a large nonstick skillet over medium-high heat. Season the scallops with salt to taste. Add the scallops to the skillet and cook until the bacon is browned on one side, about 3 minutes. Turn and brown the other side, about 2 minutes longer. Using a slotted spoon, transfer to paper towels to drain briefly.

7. To serve, spoon an equal amount of the bean purée in the center of each of 4 dinner plates. Top each with a scallop, then the leek, and drizzle the Cilantro Oil around the plate.

WINE NOTES

This dish has four taste elements: the sweetness of the scallop, the smokiness of the bacon, the earthiness of the beans, and the heat of the morita chiles. This requires a light to medium-bodied but aromatic white such as an Arneis from Piedmont. Especially good with this dish is Ceretto's Blangè Arneis. Try to find the most recent vintage.

nopales rellenos con mariscos y chipotle
grilled cactus and seafood napoleons with chipotle cream

Fresh nopales, or cactus leaves, grilled until just tender, are an unusual ingredient for most Americans, and they are sure to start a conversation at your dinner party. This wonderful first course is really a kind of sandwich with luscious shrimp and crab in a smoky-spicy chipotle cream layered between two nopales. **MAKES 4 SERVINGS**

8 small nopales (cactus leaves)

Olive oil for brushing

Fine sea salt

CHIPOTLE SEAFOOD SAUCE

1 tablespoon unsalted butter

⅓ cup finely chopped white onion

6 canned chipotles in adobo, including clinging adobo sauce

2 cups heavy cream

8 ounces medium shrimp, shelled and deveined

8 ounces fresh lump crabmeat, preferably blue crab, picked over for shell

Fine sea salt

4 cilantro sprigs for garnish

1. Prepare a hot fire in a charcoal grill or preheat a gas grill to high. While the grill is heating, prepare the nopales: Remove any cactus thorns with tweezers, pliers, or a small knife. Lightly brush the nopales with olive oil and season with salt to taste. Lightly oil the grill grids. Place the nopales on the grill and cover. Grill, turning occasionally, until tender and well marked by the grill, about 4 minutes. Transfer to a plate and keep warm.

2. To make the Chipotle Seafood Sauce: Melt the butter in a medium saucepan over medium heat. Add the onion and cook, stirring often, until translucent, about 4 minutes. Meanwhile, purée the chipotles with 1 cup of the cream in a blender. Strain through a fine-meshed sieve into a medium bowl, adding the remaining 1 cup cream. Add the chipotle cream to the onion and bring to a boil in a large saucepan over high heat, taking care that the cream does not boil over. Reduce the heat to medium and stir constantly with a wooden spoon until the cream is thick enough to coat the spoon, about 6 minutes. (The sauce can be prepared up to 2 hours ahead and kept at room temperature. Return to a simmer before proceeding.) Add the shrimp and cook just until they begin to turn opaque around the edges, about 2 minutes. Add the crab and cook just until it is heated through, about 1 minute. Season with salt to taste.

3. To serve, place 1 nopal in the center of each of 4 dinner plates. Spoon equal amounts of the seafood sauce over each nopal, reserving about ¼ cup of the sauce in the pan. Top each with another nopal, drizzle with the remaining cream sauce, and garnish with the cilantro. Serve immediately.

WINE NOTES
Even though the sauce on this dish contains chipotle chiles, the cream tempers the heat. A good wine to match would be a ripe-style California Chardonnay with restrained oak such as those made by Au Bon Climat or Cakebread.

langostinos con salsa verde cruda
langoustines with "raw" green salsa

Langoustines, also called Dublin Bay prawns, look and taste like miniature lobsters, and their natural sweetness is enhanced by other somewhat sweet ingredients like corn. Here they are wrapped in an unusual crust of very thin strips of sweet potatoes and sautéed for a striking presentation. If you wish, substitute colossal shrimp, sometimes labeled U-15 (to indicate that there are fewer than 15 shrimp to the pound), for the langoustines. You will need a turning slicer (see Note) to cut the sweet potato. MAKES 4 SERVINGS

1 large sweet potato (if making with shrimp, use 2 medium sweet potatoes), peeled

4 langoustines, shelled, heads and feelers removed, or 8 colossal (U-15) shrimp, shelled and deveined

GREEN SALSA

2 ears corn, kernels cut from the cob (about 1 cup)

4 tomatillos, husked, rinsed, and finely diced

1 serrano chile, sliced into thin rounds

12 cilantro sprigs

Fine sea salt

½ cup olive oil

Fine sea salt

⅓ cup all-purpose flour

8 grape tomatoes, halved lengthwise, for garnish

Chile Oil (page 139)

1. Using a turning slicer (see Note), cut the sweet potato into long, thin shreds. Working one at a time, wind sweet potato shreds around each shellfish as needed to cover it in a single layer, and secure the sweet potato shreds in place with a food pick. Transfer to a plate, cover with plastic wrap, and refrigerate for up to 8 hours. (Sweet potatoes do not discolor like regular potatoes.)

2. To make the salsa: Bring a small saucepan of lightly salted water to a boil over high heat. Add the corn kernels and cook just until they turn bright yellow, about 2 minutes. Drain in a sieve and rinse with cold water to stop the cooking. Purée the tomatillos, chile, and cilantro in a food processor or blender, adding a tablespoon or two of water, if needed. Transfer to a bowl and stir in the corn. Season with salt to taste. (The salsa can be made up to 8 hours ahead and stored at room temperature.)

3. Heat the olive oil in a large, heavy skillet over medium heat until it shimmers. Season the shellfish with salt to taste. Put the flour in a shallow bowl. Dredge the shellfish in the flour and shake off the excess. Carefully place the shellfish in the oil. For langoustines, cook until golden on the bottom, about 3 minutes, then turn and cook until golden on the other side, about 2 minutes longer. If using shrimp, increase the heat to medium-high and cook until golden, about 2 minutes per side. Using a slotted

spatula, transfer the shellfish to paper towels to drain briefly, then carefully remove and discard the food picks.

4. To serve, spoon equal amounts of the salsa in the center of each of 4 dinner plates. Top each with a prawn or 2 shrimp. Garnish each with 4 tomato halves and drizzle Chile Oil around the edge of the plate. Serve immediately.

NOTE: To make the long shreds of sweet potatoes, you will need a turning slicer, available at well-stocked kitchenware shops and online (see Sources, page 187). This manual appliance will be a useful tool in your kitchen and can be put into action to shred other hard vegetables into professional-looking garnishes and salads, such as the beet strings on page 44. While there are top-of-the-line models for restaurant kitchens, Benriner makes a good, moderately priced version.

WINE NOTES
The richness of the langoustines and the spiciness of the tomatillo-corn relish is complemented well by an Austrian old-vine Riesling such as those produced by Allram, Hirsch, or Nigl.

seviche de pescado clásico
fish seviche

Seviche is one of the glories of Mexican cuisine. This version is stripped to the essentials: fresh citrus juice to marinate the fish, bright tomato salsa for vibrant color and flavor, and smooth avocado for textural contrast. I prefer marlin for my seviche, but sea bass, snapper, swordfish, or any other relatively firm fish will do, as long as it is very fresh. MAKES 4 SERVINGS

8 ounces firm-textured fish fillets, such as marlin, skinned and cut into ¼-inch dice

1 cup fresh lime juice, plus more if needed

Salsa Mexicana (page 48)

1 ripe avocado, peeled, pitted, and thinly sliced, for garnish

Cilantro sprigs for garnish

Tortilla chips for serving

1. Put the fish in a medium glass or stainless-steel bowl. (Do not use aluminum, copper, or ceramic bowls, as they may react with the lime juice.) Add the lime juice and stir gently to coat the fish, adding more juice to completely submerge the fish, if needed. Cover with plastic wrap and refrigerate until the fish is opaque throughout (cut a piece of fish in half to check), about 4 hours.

2. Drain the fish in a colander, discarding the juice. Return to the bowl, add the Salsa Mexicana, and stir gently. Cover and refrigerate for at least 1 hour or up to 4 hours to blend the flavors.

3. To serve, spoon the seviche into glass serving bowls. Garnish with the avocado and cilantro. Serve with the tortilla chips.

WINE NOTES

The marlin, lime juice, cilantro, and onions in this dish pair well with a Vermentino from Bolgheri, Italy. In particular, the medium-bodied, lemony, floral-scented version from Guado al Tasso, produced by Antinori, is excellent. Also, a Grüner Veltliner from Austria has a natural affinity with fresh tomatoes. Try one by Hirsch, Nigl, or Allram. Try to find the most recent vintage of either a Vermintino or Grüner Veltliner.

seviche de langosta con naranjas y serranos
lobster seviche with oranges and serranos

While seviche can be nothing more than citrus-marinated fish, this more elegant version is made luxurious with lobster and an undercurrent of tequila and chiles. As a final fillip, a silky avocado mousse (really a light purée) ties it all together. For a finished look, the ingredients are stacked with the help of a square stainless-steel entremets mold (see Sources, page 187), but a round custard cup or ramekin will work well, too. If your fishmonger sells shelled lobster meat, you can skip cooking and shelling the lobster tails. MAKES 4 SERVINGS

2½ pounds thawed frozen lobster tails, or 1 pound cooked lobster meat

1½ cups fresh orange juice, strained

¼ cup fresh lime juice, strained

¼ cup silver tequila, preferably 100% agave

3 ripe plum (Roma) tomatoes, peeled, seeded (see page 26), and diced (about 1½ cups)

⅓ cup pitted and finely chopped manzanilla olives

½ cup thinly sliced scallions (about 3 large scallions, including part of the greens)

½ cup finely chopped fresh cilantro

1 tablespoon seeded and minced serrano or jalapeño chile

½ teaspoon fine sea salt

AVOCADO MOUSSE

1 ripe avocado, peeled and pitted

2 to 3 teaspoons fresh lime juice

Fine sea salt

½ cup microgreens for garnish

Chile Oil (page 139) for garnish

Tortilla chips for serving (optional)

1. Bring a large saucepan of lightly salted water to a boil. Add the lobster tails and cook until the shells turn red, about 5 minutes. Drain and let cool. Remove the lobster meat from the shells and coarsely chop the meat. If the lobster seems slightly undercooked, don't worry.

2. Mix the orange juice, lime juice, tequila, tomatoes, olives, scallions, cilantro, chile, and salt in a medium glass or stainless-steel bowl. (Do not use aluminum, copper, or ceramic bowls, as they may react with the lime juice.) Stir in the lobster meat, cover, and refrigerate for at least 2 hours or up to 3 hours for the flavors to marry.

3. Just before serving, make the Avocado Mousse: Using a hand blender, purée the avocado and 1 teaspoon of the lime juice in a small bowl until the avocado is light and airy. Add salt and additional lime juice to taste. (The Avocado Mousse can be made up to 30 minutes before using, but no longer.)

4. Drain the seviche in a sieve. Place a 2- to 2½-inch-square entremets mold in the center of a chilled dinner plate. Put one-fourth of the Avocado Mousse in the mold and spread with a small spatula. Top with one-fourth of the lobster seviche. Carefully remove the mold. Repeat with the remaining ingredients on 3 more chilled plates. Garnish the top of each seviche with a sprinkle of microgreens, then drizzle Chile Oil around the edge of each plate. Serve immediately, with tortilla chips, if you wish.

WINE NOTES

The manzanilla olives and silver tequila add a strong herbal note to this dish, which pairs well with Sauvignon Blanc, but the lobster calls for something a little richer. An excellent compromise is a Sauvignon Blanc/Sémillon blend, and a wonderful example of this is the Novelist by Cosentino. A recent vintage would be best.

camarones al carbón con dos salsas
grilled shrimp with two sauces

With two sauces, both as vibrantly flavored as they are brightly colored, a dish as simple as grilled shrimp becomes extraordinary. Make the sauces well ahead of serving, and this appetizer will come together in no time.

MAKES 6 SERVINGS

24 extra-large (16 to 20 count) shrimp, preferably tiger shrimp, shelled and deveined, tails intact

¼ cup olive oil

Fine sea salt

1 cup Avocado-Tomatillo Sauce (page 162)

1 cup Roasted Tomato–Chipotle Sauce (page 161)

2 mangos, peeled, pitted, and cut into 24 thin slices (see Note)

1. Prepare a hot fire in a charcoal grill or preheat a gas grill to high.

2. Mix the shrimp, olive oil, and salt to taste in a large bowl. Place the shrimp on the grill and cook, turning occasionally, just until opaque, about 4 minutes. (The shrimp may also be broiled.)

3. Spread a scant 3 tablespoons of the Avocado-Tomatillo Sauce over half of a dinner plate, then a scant 3 tablespoons of the Roasted Tomato–Chipotle sauce to cover the other half. Arrange 4 shrimp down the center of the plate between the two sauces. Garnish with 4 mango slices placed at angles to the shrimp (2, 4, 8, and 10 o'clock). Repeat with the remaining ingredients on 5 more dinner plates. Serve immediately.

NOTE: Peeling and pitting mangoes is not difficult, as long as you remember that the flattened, elongated pit runs lengthwise through the fruit. Be sure that the fruit is ripe—it should yield slightly when squeezed, and the skin may be freckled with dark spots. Above all, it should be sweetly perfumed. Place the mango on its side on a work surface. The pit, which is about ½ inch thick, runs horizontally through the center of the fruit. Use a sharp knife to cut off the top of the fruit just above the top of the pit. Turn the mango over and cut off the other side of the fruit. Using a large metal serving spoon, scoop the mango flesh from each portion in one piece. The peeled mango can now be chopped or sliced as required. The pit portion can be pared with a small knife, and the flesh nibbled from the pit as the cook's treat.

WINE NOTES

The big flavors of the chipotle-tomato and the avocado-tomatillo sauces scream for bold wines. Viognier immediately comes to mind. Either a young Condrieu from Guigal from the northern Rhône or a California version such as those made by Arrowood and Calera will pair well.

tortas de jaiba con salsa de aguacate y habanero
crab cakes with avocado-habanero sauce

Crab cakes don't have to be from New England to be tasty—serrano chiles, cilantro, and tomatillos increase the flavor profile of these Mexican-style cakes immensely. Fresh crabmeat is always best; pasteurized crab is easily attainable at price clubs and the like, but it isn't quite as sweet as the fresh. These seasonings definitely do improve pasteurized crabmeat, though. If you have the time, serve these as I do at ¡Salpicón!, garnished with frizzled beets and onions and drops of beet juice, but rest assured that the crab cakes and sauce will be great without them. MAKES 6 SERVINGS

MARINATED CARROT

1 large carrot, peeled

3 tablespoons cider vinegar

Pinch of fine sea salt

CRAB CAKES

1 pound fresh lump crabmeat, picked over for shell

4 small tomatillos, husked, rinsed, and finely chopped (½ cup)

⅓ cup chopped fresh cilantro

3 tablespoons thinly sliced scallion, including green parts

1 tablespoon finely chopped celery

1 tablespoon seeded and minced serrano chile

¼ teaspoon fine sea salt

2 large eggs, beaten

2 cups panko (Japanese bread crumbs)

½ cup olive oil

AVOCADO-HABANERO SAUCE

1 cup Avocado-Tomatillo Sauce (page 162)

1 habanero chile, seeded, deveined, and minced, or to taste

BEET AND ONION STRINGS (recipe follows) for garnish (optional)

BEET JUICE (recipe follows) for garnish (optional)

1. To marinate the carrot: Pressing hard with a vegetable peeler, cut the carrot into paper-thin slices. Toss the carrot strips, vinegar, and salt in a small glass or stainless-steel bowl. Cover and refrigerate for at least 1 hour or up to 12 hours.

2. To make the crab cakes: Put the crabmeat in a large bowl. Mix the tomatillos, cilantro, scallion, celery, chile, and salt in a small bowl (this will mix them more efficiently than adding them separately to the crab) and add to the crab. Add the eggs and 1 cup of the panko and mix gently. Shape the crabmeat mixture into 6 cakes about 1 inch thick (use a 2½-inch entremets mold, if you wish). Gently coat the crab cakes on both sides with the remaining 1 cup panko.

3. Heat the oil in a large nonstick skillet or sauté pan over medium-high heat until it shimmers. In batches, add the crab cakes and cook until lightly browned on the bottom, about 1 minute. Turn and brown the other side. Using a slotted spatula, transfer to paper towels to drain, then place on a baking sheet. (The crab cakes can be prepared to this point up to 6 hours ahead, loosely covered with plastic wrap, and refrigerated.)

4. To make the sauce: Put the Avocado-Tomatillo Sauce in a small bowl and stir in the chile a little at a time until the sauce is as hot as you like. Cover and set aside at room temperature for up to 1 hour.

5. Position a rack in the top third of the oven and preheat the oven to 375°F. Bake the crab cakes until heated through, 7 to 10 minutes.

6. To serve, spoon about ⅙ cup of the Avocado-Habanero Sauce in the center of a dinner plate and top with a crab cake. Top with 3 marinated carrot slices, then some fried Beet and Onion Strings, if using. Squeeze droplets of Beet Juice around each crab cake. Repeat with the remaining ingredients on 5 more plates. Serve immediately.

WINE NOTES

To let the sweetness of the crab shine through while balancing the heat from the Avocado-Habanero Sauce, an unoaked Riesling with pure and crisp fruit such as Grosset's Polish Hill Riesling from the Clare Valley in Australia is perfect (although just about any dry-style Riesling would be fine).

BEET AND ONION STRINGS: You will need a turning slicer (see Note, page 34) to make these. Shred 1 peeled large red beet into very thin strings on a turning slicer. Transfer to a medium bowl and toss with ¼ cup all-purpose flour to coat the beet strings. Pour enough vegetable oil into a heavy, medium saucepan to come halfway up the sides and heat over high heat to 375°F (check temperature with a candy thermometer). In batches, shake off the excess flour from the beets and deep-fry in the oil until crisp and golden brown, about 2 minutes. Using a wire-mesh skimmer, transfer the beet strips to paper towels to drain. Keep warm in a preheated 200°F oven while frying the onions. Cut 1 white onion in half, then into very thin half-moons. Toss in a bowl with ¼ cup all-purpose flour to coat. Return the same oil to 375°F. In batches, shaking off the excess flour, deep-fry the onion strings until golden brown, about 3 minutes.

BEET JUICE: Using a vegetable juicer, extract the juice from 1 peeled large red beet. (Or, blend the beet, coarsely chopped, in a blender with a tablespoon or two of water until puréed.) Strain the juice through a fine-meshed sieve into a small saucepan. Bring the juice to a boil over medium-high heat. Sprinkle 1 teaspoon cornstarch over 1 tablespoon cold water in a small bowl and stir to dissolve the cornstarch. Whisk into the boiling beet juice and cook until thickened. Let cool completely. (The beet juice can be made up to 3 days ahead, covered and refrigerated.) Transfer to a plastic squeeze bottle.

tártaro de salmón curado al tequila y atún
tequila-cured salmon tartare with tuna

Tequila does more than add its distinctive taste to the cured salmon—the alcohol enhances and heightens the other flavors, too. Diced apple adds a surprising crunch to the tender fish. Use a light-bodied silver tequila here, and save the richer ones for sipping. MAKES 4 SERVINGS

TEQUILA-CURED SALMON

8 ounces wild salmon fillet, preferably sockeye

½ cup chopped fresh cilantro

½ cup kosher salt

⅓ cup silver tequila

¼ cup packed light brown sugar

CHILE CREAM

½ cup sour cream

½ teaspoon seeded and minced serrano chile

Pinch of fine sea salt

½ green apple, peeled, cored, and cut into ¼-inch dice

⅓ cup plus 1 tablespoon fresh lime juice

5 ounces tuna steak, preferably ahi, cut into ½-inch dice

2 tablespoons extra-virgin olive oil

2 teaspoons finely chopped fresh chives

1 teaspoon seeded and minced chile de árbol or serrano chile

Fine sea salt

½ ripe avocado, peeled, pitted, and diced

Microgreens for serving (optional)

1. To make the cured salmon: Using a thin, flexible knife, cut off and discard the skin from the salmon. Pull out any pin bones. Mix the cilantro, salt, tequila, and brown sugar in a small bowl and rub the mixture all over the salmon. Wrap the salmon in a double thickness of plastic wrap. Place on a rimmed baking sheet and top with a heavy skillet. Refrigerate the salmon for at least 8 hours or up to 24 hours, flipping the fish at least 4 times.

2. Unwrap the salmon and remove the cilantro with a kitchen brush. Cut the cured salmon into ½-inch dice. Transfer to a bowl, cover, and refrigerate until ready to use.

3. To make the Chile Cream: Blend the sour cream, chile, and salt in a small food processor (or process in a small bowl with a hand blender). Rub through a fine-meshed sieve into a small bowl. Cover and refrigerate until using. (The cream can be made up to 1 day ahead.)

4. Toss the apple with the ⅓ cup lime juice in a small glass bowl. Cover and refrigerate for at least 30 minutes or up to 4 hours.

5. When ready to serve, drain the apple. Mix the salmon, tuna, drained apple, olive oil, chives, chile, and the 1 tablespoon lime juice and season with salt to taste. Lightly mix in the avocado, taking care not to break it up.

6. Place a 2½-inch entremets mold on a chilled dinner plate. Fill with about one-fourth of the fish tartare, then carefully remove the mold. (Or, fill an oiled ¾-cup custard cup or ramekin with the fish tartare and invert it onto the plate.) Drizzle the Chile Cream around the fish tartare, then top with the microgreens. Repeat with the remaining ingredients on 3 more chilled plates. Serve immediately.

WINE NOTES

The richness of this dish is complemented well with a sparkling wine, in particular a rosé Champagne from any number of houses. Veuve Clicquot, Krug, Laurent-Perrier, and Billecart-Salmon all are fine choices. For domestic sparklers, look for Schramsberg, Chandon, or Scharffenberger.

guacamole picado
"chopped" guacamole

Some recipes for guacamole are made in a blender or food processor, but this is as wrong as can be. Guacamole should be pleasantly lumpy. While you can make it by chopping and mixing the various ingredients, I simply combine Salsa Mexicana (which includes the required guacamole seasonings like onions, lime, chiles, and cilantro) into the avocados. For those who want more heat, serve Árbol Chile Sauce (page 158) alongside. MAKES 4 SERVINGS

SALSA MEXICANA

3 plum (Roma) tomatoes, seeded (see page 26) and diced (1 cup)

¼ cup finely chopped white onion

¼ cup finely chopped fresh cilantro

1 tablespoon seeded and finely chopped serrano or jalapeño chile

1 tablespoon extra-virgin olive oil

1 tablespoon fresh lime juice

Fine sea salt to taste

2 ripe avocados, peeled, pitted, and diced

Fine sea salt

Tortilla chips for serving

Árbol Chile Sauce (page 158) for serving

1. To make the salsa: Mix all of the ingredients in a medium bowl. Cover and let stand at room temperature for at least 20 minutes or up to 2 hours. Drain before using, reserving the liquid.

2. Add the diced avocado to the Salsa Mexicana and stir gently to blend. Season with salt to taste. If needed, adjust the seasoning with the reserved salsa liquid. Cover and refrigerate for at least 1 hour or up to 8 hours to marry the flavors.

3. Remove from refrigerator 30 minutes before serving. Serve with tortilla chips and a bowl of Árbol Chile Sauce passed on the side.

WINE NOTES

This is one dish that is excellent paired with tequila. Either a blanco margarita or a chilled blanco (silver tequila) to sip would be excellent. But if you want to stick to wine, feel free. The richness of the avocado and the tanginess of the tomatoes in the salsa demand that the accompanying wine be of medium-weight but with high acidity. Normally, Pinot Grigio would not be my first choice, but Livio Felluga from Alto Adige, Italy, makes a rich but crisp version. If you're in the mood for red, Sangiovese is a great match, especially Badia a Coltibuono's Chianti Classico or Il Borro's Polissena, both from Tuscany.

jalapeños rellenos de queso chihuahua
stuffed jalapeños with chihuahua cheese

These bear no resemblance to the frozen stuffed jalapeños that you might find at a fast-food place. They are not snacks, but a first-class first course of lightly battered cheese-filled chiles served in a smooth black bean purée. **MAKES 6 SERVINGS**

BLACK BEAN SAUCE

1 cup dried black beans, rinsed and picked over

½ teaspoon sea salt

STUFFED JALAPEÑOS

18 jalapeño chiles, roasted and peeled (see page 22)

2 cups (8 ounces) shredded Chihuahua or Monterey Jack cheese

Canola oil for frying

5 large egg whites

½ teaspoon sea salt

1 cup all-purpose flour

GARNISH

½ cup Mexican crema or crème fraîche in a squeeze bottle

2 ripe avocados, peeled, pitted, and cut lengthwise into 9 slices each

1 plum (Roma) tomato, peeled, seeded (see page 26), and diced

18 fresh cilantro leaves

Warm corn tortillas for serving

1. To make the Black Bean Sauce: Bring 3 quarts of water to a boil in a large saucepan over high heat. Add the beans and return to a boil. Reduce the heat to medium-low and simmer the beans for 1 hour. Add the salt and cook until very tender, about 30 minutes more. Drain the beans in a colander, reserving the cooking liquid. Process the beans in a blender or food processor, adding the reserved cooking liquid as needed to make a smooth, somewhat runny purée. (The purée can be made, cooled, covered, and refrigerated up to 1 day ahead. If making ahead, cover and refrigerate the cooking liquid as well. Reheat the purée over low heat, adding the cooking liquid as needed to return the purée to a runny consistency.)

2. To prepare the jalapeños: Make a lengthwise cut on one side of each chile and remove the seeds. Stuff each chile with some cheese, then close the cut with a food pick. Cover and refrigerate the chiles until ready to use, up to 4 hours. Remove the chiles from the refrigerator 30 minutes before frying. (If the chiles are chilled, they could make the oil bubble over.)

3. Position a rack in the center of the oven and preheat the oven to 200°F. Line a baking sheet with a double thickness of paper towels. Add oil to a large, heavy skillet to a depth of ½ inch. Heat over high heat until the oil is shimmering but not smoking. Meanwhile, beat the egg whites in a large, grease-free bowl with an electric mixer on low speed until foamy. Add the salt and beat on high speed until soft peaks form. Put the flour in a shallow dish. Working in batches, coat the chiles in flour, shake off the excess flour, then dip them in the egg white. Carefully place the chiles in the hot oil and fry, turning them once, until golden, about 3 minutes. Using a slotted spoon or wire-mesh skimmer, transfer to the paper towels to drain, and keep warm in the oven while frying the remaining chiles.

4. To serve, spread one-sixth of the bean purée into a round on a dinner plate. Squeeze 2 or 3 concentric circles of *crema* on the purée. Starting at the 12 o'clock point on the purée round, draw the tip of a sharp knife from the edge of the purée into the center. Repeat at 2, 4, 6, 8, and 10 o'clock points to make a weblike design. Garnish with 3 avocado slices placed at 12, 4, and 8 o'clock, then place 1 chile between each avocado slice. Place some diced tomato in the center, then top each chile with a cilantro leaf. Repeat to make a total of 6 servings. Serve immediately, with the tortillas.

WINE NOTES

With this dish, you need a wine that will cut the heat from the chiles while complementing the creaminess of the cheese and the earthiness of the beans. One of my favorite pairings is with Albariño, in particular one from Pazo de Señoráns or Martín Códax from the Rías Baixas.

portobellos enchipotlados a la parrilla
grilled portobellos with chipotle sauce

Pineapple juice may sound like an unusual marinade for grilled portobellos, but the sweet-and-sour juice is actually the perfect foil for the meaty texture and earthy flavor of this mushroom. And as hot as chipotle chiles are, they have an underlying sweetness that plays with the fruity pineapple (don't forget that chiles are fruits, too). While I serve this as a first course at ¡Salpicón!, it would make a nice vegetarian entrée for two. MAKES 4 SERVINGS

4 portobello mushrooms, stemmed and wiped clean with a wet paper towel

4 cups canned unsweetened pineapple juice

1 cup diced fresh pineapple

1 cup julienned jícama

1 cup Roasted Tomato–Chipotle Sauce (page 161)

½ cup finely chopped fresh cilantro, plus 4 cilantro sprigs for garnish

Fine sea salt

1. Put the mushrooms in a baking dish or a self-sealing plastic bag and add the pineapple juice. Cover (or close the bag) and refrigerate for at least 4 hours or up to 8 hours. Remove the mushrooms from the juice and let stand at room temperature for about 30 minutes before grilling.

2. Prepare a medium-hot fire in a charcoal grill or preheat a gas grill to medium. Lightly oil the grill grids. Place the mushrooms on the grill, smooth sides down, and cover the grill. Cook until the mushrooms begin to give off juices, about 5 minutes. Turn, re-cover the grill, and cook until the mushrooms are tender, about 3 minutes longer. Transfer to a plate and cover with aluminum foil to keep warm.

3. Just before serving, mix the pineapple, jícama, ½ cup of the Roasted Tomato–Chipotle Sauce, the chopped cilantro, and salt to taste in a medium bowl. If you wish, cut each mushroom cap into ½-inch-thick slices. To serve, place a mushroom (either whole or with the slices fanned out) on each of 4 plates. Top with equal amounts of the pineapple mixture, then spoon the remaining Roasted Tomato–Chipotle Sauce around the mushrooms. Garnish each serving with a cilantro sprig and serve immediately.

WINE NOTES

A full-bodied white wine with good acidity is needed here to complement the portobellos, but in order to handle the tomato-chipotle sauce, unoaked wine works best. The pineapple adds a hint of sweetness as well as spice notes, so a Gewürztraminer from Alsace is perfect for this dish. Any number of producers would work, but look for Hugel, Zind-Humbrecht, León Beyer, and Domaine Ostertag.

poblanos rellenos con papas y aguacate
stuffed poblano chiles with avocado and potatoes

What a wonderful dish this is, full of unexpected flavors and textures. Roasted poblano chiles are stuffed with mashed potatoes and avocados, then marinated in a sweet-and-sour mixture seasoned with roasted garlic. MAKES 6 SERVINGS

2 unpeeled baking potatoes, scrubbed

6 poblano chiles, roasted and peeled (see page 22)

3 avocados, peeled, pitted, and coarsely mashed

3 tablespoons olive oil

½ tablespoon black peppercorns, freshly ground

Fine sea salt

ROASTED GARLIC CLOVES

18 plump garlic cloves

1 cup skim milk

1 tablespoon olive oil

MARINADE

1½ cups water

3 small cones piloncillo (Mexican raw sugar), crushed with a meat mallet, or 6 tablespoons packed dark brown sugar

¼ cup olive oil

1 large yellow onion, halved, peeled, and thinly sliced

2 cups cider vinegar

1 teaspoon dried Mexican oregano

1 teaspoon black peppercorns

8 cloves

6 allspice berries

4 bay leaves

1. Put the potatoes in a medium saucepan and add lightly salted water to cover. Bring to a boil over high heat. Reduce the heat to medium-low and cook until the potatoes are tender, about 30 minutes. Drain and let stand until cool enough to handle. Peel the potatoes and place in a medium bowl. Mash the potatoes, leaving them a bit lumpy.

2. Make a lengthwise cut in each chile and remove the seeds. Combine the mashed potatoes, avocados, olive oil, and ground peppercorns in a medium bowl and season with salt to taste. Stuff the chiles with the potato mixture. Place in a 9-by-13-inch baking dish. Cover with plastic wrap and refrigerate.

3. To roast the garlic: Position a rack in the center of the oven and preheat the oven to 350°F. Bring the garlic and milk to a boil in a medium saucepan over medium heat, then boil for 3 minutes, taking care that the milk does not boil over. Drain the garlic in a sieve, discarding the milk. In a small bowl, toss the garlic cloves in the olive oil. Spread the garlic in a single layer on a baking sheet and cover with aluminum foil. Roast until tender and golden, about 20 minutes. Set aside.

4. To make the marinade: Bring the water and piloncillo or brown sugar to a boil in a small saucepan over high heat. Boil, stirring often, until the sugar is dissolved and the water is reduced to 1 cup, about 5 minutes. Remove from the heat.

5. Heat the oil in a medium skillet over medium heat. Add the onion and cook until it begins to soften, about 1 minute. Add the sugar water, vinegar, oregano, peppercorns, cloves, allspice, and bay leaves and bring to a simmer (do not boil). Remove from the heat, add the roasted garlic, and let cool completely. Pour the marinade over the chiles, cover, and refrigerate for at least 6 hours or up to 12 hours.

6. To serve, remove the chiles from the refrigerator and let come to room temperature. Place a single chile on each of 6 plates, along with some of the marinade, including some of the onion and garlic cloves.

WINE NOTES
Since this dish is sauced with an escabèche (a sweet, spiced vinaigrette), one of the best matches is a German Riesling from the Mosel, such as Carl Schmitt-Wagner's Kabinett Riesling.

flores de calabaza con queso de cabra
squash blossoms stuffed with goat cheese

When I first came to Chicago, I never dreamed that I would one day be able to buy the squash blossoms that I loved back in Mexico. I was thrilled when my produce provider brought some in, and I immediately made my favorite dishes, like quesadillas, soup, and scrambled eggs, with squash blossoms—all of which use the blossoms by the handful. When I put them on ¡Salpicón!'s menu, I chose a recipe that uses individual blossoms, stuffed with goat cheese and herbs, then battered and fried. You should be able to find squash blossoms at your local farmers' market in July and August, or ask a neighbor with a backyard patch of zucchini or pumpkin.

MAKES 4 SERVINGS

½ cup crumbled fresh
goat cheese

¼ cup finely chopped fresh
epazote, oregano, or basil

Fine sea salt

8 large squash blossoms

CORN RELISH

1 ear corn, kernels cut off (½ cup)

1 serrano chile, seeded, deveined,
and finely chopped

1 cup cake flour

¼ cup cornstarch

½ teaspoon baking soda

½ teaspoon sea salt

¾ cup olive oil

1 cup chilled club soda

1 cup Roasted Poblano Cream
Sauce (page 169), warmed

Fresh epazote, oregano, or basil
leaves for garnish

1. Mix the goat cheese and herb in a small bowl and season with salt to taste.

2. Remove the sepals of one squash blossom. Make a long incision along one side of the blossom and remove the stamen. Using a teaspoon, stuff the inside of the blossom with about 1 tablespoon of the goat cheese mixture and close tightly, using the natural moisture of the cheese to close the blossom. Repeat with the remaining blossoms. (The blossoms can be prepared up to 8 hours ahead, covered and refrigerated. Remove from the refrigerator 30 minutes before serving.)

3. To make the Corn Relish: Bring 2 cups of salted water to a boil in a small saucepan over high heat. Add the corn, reduce the heat to medium, and cook until the corn is tender, about 4 minutes. Drain. Transfer to a bowl and mix in the chile. (The salsa can be made up to 4 hours ahead, covered and stored at room temperature.)

4. To start the batter: Sift the cake flour, cornstarch, baking soda, and salt together into a large, shallow bowl.

5. Position the rack in the center of the oven and preheat the oven to 200°F. Line a baking sheet with a double thickness of paper towels. Heat the oil in a large skillet over medium-high heat until the oil is shimmering. Mix the club soda into the flour mixture and stir until well combined. Working in batches, dip the stuffed squash blossoms one at a time into the batter, shaking off the excess batter. Add to the pan and sauté, turning the blossoms once, until golden brown and crisp, about 2 minutes per side. Using a slotted spoon, transfer to the paper towels. Keep warm in the oven while frying the remaining blossoms.

6. To serve, spoon about ¼ cup Roasted Poblano Cream Sauce in the center of each of 4 plates. Place 2 squash blossoms on the plate. Garnish with the Corn Relish and herb leaves. Serve immediately.

WINE NOTES
The goat cheese in the squash blossoms calls for Sauvignon Blanc. Lucien Crochet's Sancerre from the Loire Valley and Villa María's Sauvignon Blanc from New Zealand are equally delicious here.

salpicón de carne
cold marinated beef brisket

This is the dish from central Mexico for which the restaurant is named. I love it with beef brisket, the sturdy cut of meat cooked until meltingly tender. There are also versions of salpicón with chicken or shrimp (I even make it with crabmeat), but in these cases, the cooking times are much shorter.   MAKES 4 SERVINGS

BRISKET

2 pounds beef brisket, trimmed and cut into 2-inch pieces

½ yellow onion, cut into quarters

4 garlic cloves, crushed

4 thyme sprigs

1 tablespoon fine sea salt

CHIPOTLE VINAIGRETTE

¾ cup extra-virgin olive oil

⅓ cup apple cider vinegar

2 tablespoons canned adobo sauce from chipotle chiles (below)

1 tablespoon dried Mexican oregano

Fine sea salt

1 large baking potato, peeled and cut into ¼-inch dice

½ small red onion, thinly sliced

6 canned chipotle chiles in adobo, cut into strips

Fine sea salt

8 grape tomatoes, halved

1 ripe avocado, peeled, pitted, and sliced

Tortilla chips for serving

1. To cook the brisket: Bring 5 quarts of water to a boil in a large stockpot. Add the beef, onion, garlic, thyme, and salt and return to a boil. Reduce the heat to medium-low. Simmer, uncovered, until the meat is very tender, 1½ to 2 hours. Drain the meat in a colander, discarding the onion and garlic, and let cool slightly. Transfer the meat to a chopping board and shred it with 2 forks. Let cool completely. (The beef can be covered and refrigerated for up to 1 day. Bring to room temperature before continuing.)

2. To make the vinaigrette: Process the oil, vinegar, adobo, and oregano in a blender until thickened. Season with salt to taste.

3. Bring a medium saucepan of lightly salted water to a boil over high heat. Add the potato, reduce the heat to medium, and partially cover the pot. Cook until the potato is tender but not falling apart, about 20 minutes. Drain and rinse under cold water to stop the cooking. Let cool completely.

4. Just before serving, toss the shredded beef, potato, red onion, and chipotle strips with the vinaigrette in a medium bowl. Add salt to taste. Spoon equal amounts of the salpicón onto 4 plates and garnish with the tomatoes and avocado slices. Serve with tortilla chips.

WINE NOTES

The beef in this dish wants a big red wine to go with, but the chipotles say watch out! A great pairing is a California Merlot or Zinfandel. Good examples of both are made by Cosentino and Markham. Another choice would be a fruity Shiraz from Australia such as Rosemount's Diamond Label or Lindemans Bin 59. These are all full-bodied, fruit-forward wines with low tannin levels.

tinga de puerco
shredded pork with roasted tomatoes and chipotle chiles

Pork shoulder is a humble cut of meat, but it packs a lot of flavor. Here it is simmered with a chipotle-spiked tomato sauce to make a smoky-spicy topping for crisp little tortilla chips. They can be served on a plate as a first course or passed on a tray as a nibble with cocktails or beer. *Tinga* is also very good as a filling for warm corn tortillas to make soft tacos. Note that the chorizo used here is the soft, fresh Mexican kind, not the hard smoked Spanish sausage. **MAKES 32 PIECES, ABOUT 8 SERVINGS**

TOSTADITAS

8 corn tortillas

Canola oil for frying

BRAISED PORK

1 pound pork shoulder (pork butt), trimmed of fat, cut into 2-inch pieces

1 small white onion, quartered

2 garlic cloves, crushed

1 tablespoon fine sea salt

SAUCE

6 ounces Mexican chorizo, removed from casing

1 tablespoon canola oil

1 small white onion, halved and thinly sliced

2 garlic cloves, minced

2 pounds plum (Roma) tomatoes, roasted, peeled (see page 26), and chopped

2 teaspoons dried thyme

½ teaspoon ground cloves

½ teaspoon ground cinnamon

2 canned chipotle chiles in adobo, finely chopped

Fine sea salt

½ cup Mexican crema or crème fraîche in a squeeze bottle

1 ripe avocado, peeled, pitted, and diced

1. To make the tostaditas: Using a 2-inch round cookie cutter, cut 4 rounds from each tortilla. Add oil to a large skillet to a depth of ½ inch and heat over high heat until the oil is shimmering. Line a baking sheet with a double thickness of paper towels. Working in batches, add the tortillas to the oil and fry until golden brown, about 1 minute. Using a wire-mesh skimmer, transfer the tostaditas to the paper towels.

2. To braise the pork: Bring 8 cups water to boil in a large casserole or Dutch oven over high heat. Add the pork, onion, garlic, and salt and return to a boil. Reduce the heat to medium-low. Simmer, uncovered, until the pork is fork-tender, about 2 hours. Drain in a colander, discarding the onion and garlic, and let cool slightly. Transfer the pork to a chopping board and shred with 2 forks.

3. To make the sauce: Cook the chorizo in a medium nonstick skillet over low heat, stirring often and crumbling it with a wooden spoon until it turns dark red and some of the oil is released, about 15 minutes. Drain in a fine-meshed sieve to remove the excess oil, and transfer to a bowl.

4. Add the canola oil to the pan and heat over medium heat. Add the onion and cook, stirring often, until softened, about 3 minutes. Add the garlic and cook until fragrant, about 1 minute. Stir in the tomatoes, thyme, cloves, and cinnamon and bring to a simmer. Cover and reduce the heat to medium-low. Simmer until the tomatoes give off their juices, about 8 minutes. Add the chorizo, shredded pork, and chiles and mix well. Cover and simmer to blend the flavors, about 2 minutes. Remove from the heat and add salt to taste. (The pork in its sauce can be cooled, covered, and refrigerated up to 1 day ahead. Reheat slowly before serving.)

5. To serve, place 1 heaping tablespoon braised pork on each tostadita. Garnish with a drizzle of crema and a sprinkle of diced avocado. Serve hot.

WINE NOTES
Sangiovese is excellent with this dish. A Chianti Classico such as those produced by Nozzole, Querciabella, or Antinori will work well.

empanadas de picadillo
pork picadillo turnovers

Empanadas, savory turnovers stuffed with everything from tuna to pork, can be found throughout Latin America. Mine have the typical mixture of meat, spices, and a touch of sweet raisins, but I serve them with the lusty Argentine parsley sauce *chimichurri* for even more flavor impact.   MAKES 8 SERVINGS

SPICY CHIMICHURRI

¾ cup finely chopped fresh flat-leaf parsley

½ cup extra-virgin olive oil

¼ cup cider vinegar

2 tablespoons dried oregano

1 teaspoon seeded and minced serrano chile

1 teaspoon minced garlic

½ teaspoon fine sea salt

EMPANADA DOUGH

2⅔ cups all-purpose flour

½ teaspoon fine sea salt

1 cup (2 sticks) cold unsalted butter, diced

About ½ cup ice-cold water

PORK FILLING

2 teaspoons canola oil

1 small onion, finely chopped

2 garlic cloves, minced

12 ounces ground pork, as lean as possible

12 ounces ripe plum (Roma) tomatoes, finely diced, or one 14-ounce can tomatoes, drained and chopped

⅓ cup pitted and finely chopped manzanilla olives

⅓ cup raisins

⅓ cup nonpareil capers, drained and rinsed

¼ cup finely chopped natural almonds

½ teaspoon dried thyme

¼ teaspoon ground cinnamon

⅛ teaspoon ground cloves

Fine sea salt

1 egg white, beaten until foamy, for brushing

1. To make the chimichurri: Mix the parsley, oil, vinegar, oregano, chile, garlic, and salt in a medium glass or stainless-steel bowl. Cover and refrigerate for at least 6 hours or up to 12 hours. Remove from the refrigerator 1 hour before serving.

2. To make the dough: Mix the flour and salt in a large bowl, then stir in the butter. Using an electric mixer on low speed or a pastry blender, cut the butter into the flour until the mixture looks crumbly. Gradually mix in the cold water until the dough clings together. Gather into a thick disk, wrap in plastic wrap, and refrigerate for at least 1 hour or up to 4 hours.

3. To make the filling: Heat the oil in a large, heavy saucepan over medium heat. Add the onion and cook, stirring occasionally, until it softens, about 3 minutes. Stir in the garlic and cook until fragrant, about 1 minute. Add the pork and cook, stirring often and breaking up the meat with a wooden spoon, until no longer pink, about 5 minutes. Add the tomatoes and cover. Cook until the tomatoes give off their juices, about 8 minutes. Add the olives, raisins, capers, almonds, thyme, cinnamon, and cloves. Cook until the fat separates from the pork, about 20 minutes. Season with salt to taste. Let cool completely.

4. Position a rack in the center of the oven and preheat the oven to 350°F. Lightly grease a rimmed baking sheet.

5. Roll the dough out on a lightly floured surface until it is ⅛ inch thick. (If the chilled dough is too hard to roll out, let it stand at room temperature for about 15 minutes to soften slightly.) Using a saucer as a template, cut out 5-inch-diameter rounds. Gather up the scraps and roll the dough out again until you have 8 rounds. Place 1 heaping tablespoon of the pork filling into the center of a round. Fold the dough over to enclose the filling and tightly seal the edge with a fork. Transfer to the baking sheet. Repeat with the remaining rounds and filling.

6. Brush the tops of the empanadas with some of the egg white. Bake until the empanadas are nice and golden, about 15 minutes. Serve hot, with a bowl of the chimichurri passed on the side.

WINE NOTES
An especially good match for these empanadas is Cabernet Franc. I particularly enjoy a Chinon by Charles Joguet from the Loire Valley. It complements the picadillo well and provides a great counterpoint to the chimichurri sauce. A more fruit-forward version is made by Pam Starr at Crocker & Starr in Napa Valley.

tacos con hongos
mixed-mushroom tacos

This dish has so many uses, it is almost unfair to categorize it as an appetizer, even though it is a great one. While you can use whatever mushrooms are available, the recipe is especially good with the recommended combination because each has its own texture, flavor, and juiciness. Earthy and satisfying, the tacos are actually meatless, so just about any main course can follow them. But think of them too for a vegetarian entrée for dinner or brunch. And if you have the chile sauces already prepared, these tacos can also be a fast weeknight meal.   MAKES 4 TO 6 SERVINGS

¼ cup olive oil

1 large white onion, sliced

3 garlic cloves, minced

8 ounces portobello mushrooms, sliced

8 ounces cremini mushrooms, sliced

8 ounces shiitakes, stemmed and sliced

8 ounces oyster mushrooms, sliced

1 cup Guajillo Chile Purée (page 165)

1 cup Ancho Chile Purée (page 165)

Fine sea salt

¼ cup chopped fresh epazote

1 dozen corn tortillas, heated

1. Heat the oil in a large saucepan over medium-high heat. Add the onion and cook until it softens, about 3 minutes. Stir in the garlic and cook until fragrant, about 1 minute.

2. Add the portobello and cremini mushrooms, cover, and reduce the heat to medium-low. Cook, stirring occasionally, until they begin to give off their juices, about 2 minutes. Stir in the shiitakes, cover, and cook until they begin to soften, about 2 minutes. Stir in the oyster mushrooms, cover, and cook for 2 minutes longer. Stir in the Guajillo and Ancho Chile Purées and bring to a simmer. Uncover and cook, stirring often, until the sauce thickens slightly, about 10 minutes. Season with salt to taste. Stir in the epazote. (The stew can be made up to 1 day ahead, cooled, covered, and refrigerated. Reheat gently before serving.)

3. Transfer the stew to a serving bowl and serve hot, with the warm tortillas (wrap them in a clean napkin to keep warm) on the side. Allow each guest to spoon the mushroom mixture into a tortilla and roll it up before eating.

WINE NOTES
The flavors of the ancho and guajillo chiles in this dish are complemented well by an Amarone. Excellent producers are Masi, Allegrini, and Tommasi.

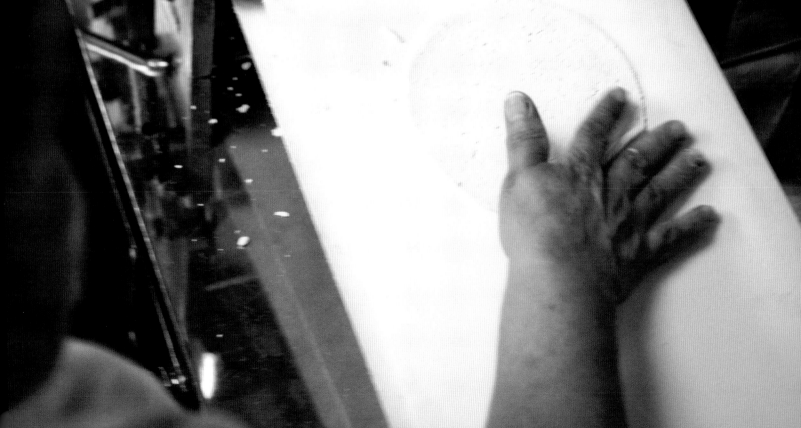

trio de tamalitos
a trio of tamales

At ¡Salpicón! we have made a specialty of our tamales, which are filled with whatever strikes my fancy on a particular day. These three, however—fresh cheese and chiles, zucchini, and black bean—are perennial favorites. If you feel ambitious and wish to replicate our trio of tamales, make a dozen of each flavor. To steam all three dozen at once, stand them up side by side in a large, wide steamer. Serve one of each flavor per guest. If you have leftovers, wrap the cooked tamales in aluminum foil and freeze for up to 1 month. Steam the frozen tamales until heated through, about 30 minutes.

If you are lucky enough to live near a tortilla factory, you can purchase fresh masa for tamales there; otherwise, you will have to make the masa from masa harina. Made from ground dried corn that has been treated with lime, masa harina comes in paper sacks, just like flour. There are two kinds. For tamales, look for the variety labeled *masa instantánea de maiz para hacer tamales* ("instant corn masa for making tamales"). The other "plain" masa harina is specifically for tortillas, but it will do in a pinch. Use about 1 pound fresh masa to replace the masa harina version. Masa is often made with lard; mine are much lighter with vegetable shortening. You can use nonhydrogenated shortening, if you wish.

tamales de frijoles negros con queso
black bean and chihuahua cheese tamales

Black beans make a double appearance here, both inside the tamales and as a sauce. Be sure the beans are cooked until they are quite tender so they blend smoothly into a purée. MAKES 12 TAMALES

BLACK BEAN PURÉE

1 cup dried black beans, rinsed and picked over

½ teaspoon fine sea salt

12 dried corn husks

MASA

½ cup vegetable shortening

1½ cups masa harina for tamales

½ cup room-temperature water

1 teaspoon baking powder

1 tablespoon fine sea salt

2 poblano chiles, roasted, peeled (see page 22), and cut into 2-by-¼-inch strips

6 ounces Chihuahua or Monterey Jack cheese, thinly sliced and cut into 2-by-¼-inch strips

1. To make the Black Bean Purée: Bring 3 quarts of water to a boil in a large saucepan over high heat. Add the beans and reduce the heat to medium-low. Simmer until the beans are almost tender, about 1 hour. Add the salt and simmer until the beans are very tender, about 30 minutes more. Drain the beans, reserving the cooking water.

2. Purée the beans in a blender, adding enough of the reserved bean cooking water as needed to make a runny, saucelike purée. Set aside.

3. Soak the corn husks in a large bowl of warm water until pliable, about 20 minutes.

4. To make the Masa: Using an electric mixer on high speed, beat the shortening in a medium bowl until creamy, about 1 minute. Add the masa harina, water, baking powder, and salt and mix on medium speed until well combined.

5. Drain the corn husks and pat dry with kitchen towels. Spread 2 or 3 tablespoons Masa in a strip about 5 inches long and 3 inches wide in the center of a corn husk. Spread about 1 tablespoon bean purée on the Masa, leaving a 1-inch border around the sides. Add 2 or 3 strips each of the poblano chile and cheese. Fold over the sides of the husk to cover the filling with Masa. Fold the top and bottom ends of the husk up and slip one end inside another to

secure the husk closed. If you wish, tie the husk closed with kitchen twine. Repeat with the remaining husks, Masa, bean purée (reserve the leftover bean purée), chile, and cheese. (The tamales and bean purée can be prepared up to 8 hours ahead, covered and refrigerated.)

6. Bring water in the bottom of a steamer to a boil. Arrange the tamales in the steamer and cover tightly. Cook until the Masa is firm and removes easily from the husk when a *tamal* is opened, about 1 hour. Check occasionally and add more boiling water to the steamer if needed.

7. Reheat the reserved bean purée in a small saucepan over medium heat until steaming. Serve the hot tamales in their husks, with the bean purée spooned over the top.

WINE NOTES
With this dish, you need a wine that will cut the heat from the chiles while complementing the creaminess of the cheese and the earthiness of the beans. One of my favorite pairings is with Albariño, in particular one from Pazo de Señoráns or Martín Códax from the Rías Baixas.

tamales de calabaza y chipotle
zucchini and chipotle tamales

These tamales, made with banana-leaf wrappers instead of corn husks, are found in the western part of Mexico. The leaves are available, fresh or frozen, at Latino and Asian markets. The filling couldn't be more simple . . . or more delicious. MAKES 12 TAMALES

Masa (facing page)

1 large zucchini, shredded

3 banana leaves, cut into twelve 4-by-15-inch rectangles

4 canned chipotle chiles in adobo, excess sauce removed, seeded and cut into 12 lengthwise strips (wear rubber gloves for this)

½ cup Mexican crema or crème fraîche

1. Put the Masa in a medium bowl. Gently fold the zucchini into the Masa.

2. Working with 1 banana leaf rectangle at a time, pass the leaf over an open flame (a gas burner or a charcoal or gas grill) until it softens and is more pliable. You can also run the leaf under an electric or gas broiler. In either case, take care not to burn the leaf, or it will taste bitter. Place the banana leaf on a work surface running lengthwise in front of you. Spread 2 or 3 tablespoons of Masa in a strip about 5 inches long and 3 inches wide and 1 inch from the bottom of the leaf. Place a chipotle strip in the center of the Masa. Fold the bottom of the leaf up to cover the filling with the Masa, then continue folding in the same direction to finish the leaf. Fold over the ends of the leaf toward the center, overlapping the ends, and tie the ends closed with kitchen twine. Repeat with the remaining leaves, Masa, and chiles. (The tamales can be prepared up to 8 hours ahead and refrigerated.)

3. Bring water in a steamer to a boil. Arrange the tamales in the steamer and cover tightly. Cook until the Masa is firm and, when a tamal is opened, the Masa removes easily from the leaf, about 1 hour. Check occasionally and add more boiling water to the steamer if needed.

4. Serve the hot tamales in their leaves (or, for a side dish, unwrap and cut each tamal into thirds), with the crema alongside.

WINE NOTES

Try these with a dry Riesling from Alsace (Josmeyer, Trimbach) or a Kabinett-level Riesling from Germany (August Kesseler, Pfeffingen).

tamales de queso fresco y chile serrano
cheese and chile tamales

These tamales sing out with essential Mexican flavors: crumbly queso fresco, zesty serrano chiles, earthy corn masa, and a rough-textured tomato salsa. MAKES 12 TAMALES

12 dried corn husks

1 teaspoon canola oil

4 serrano chiles, seeded, deveined, and cut into thin lengthwise strips

Masa (page 68)

6 ounces queso fresco or farmer's cheese, cut into twelve 1-by-1½-inch pieces

"Mortar" Salsa (page 162) for serving

½ cup Mexican crema or crème fraîche

1. Soak the corn husks in a large bowl of warm water until pliable, about 20 minutes.

2. Heat the oil in a small skillet over medium heat. Add the chiles and cook, stirring often, until softened, about 2 minutes. Using a slotted spoon, transfer the chiles to a paper towel to drain.

3. Drain the corn husks and pat dry with kitchen towels. Spread 2 or 3 tablespoons Masa in a strip about 5 inches long and 3 inches wide in the center of a corn leaf and 1 inch from the end. Top with 1 slice of cheese and a few strips of chile. Fold over the sides of the husk to cover the filling with the Masa. Fold the top and bottom ends of the husk up and slip one end inside another to close the husk. If you wish, tie the husk closed with kitchen twine. Repeat with the remaining husks, Masa, cheese, and chiles. (The tamales can be prepared up to 8 hours ahead and refrigerated.)

4. Bring water in the bottom of a steamer to a boil. Arrange the tamales in the steamer and cover tightly. Cook until the Masa is firm and removes easily from the husk when a tamal is opened, about 1 hour. Check occasionally and add more boiling water to the steamer if needed.

5. Serve the hot tamales in their husks (or, for a side dish, unwrap and cut each tamal into thirds), with the salsa and crema alongside.

WINE NOTES
Grüner Veltliner from Austria will work well with these tamales. It will cut the heat of the chiles, while complementing the tomatoes in the salsa. Try one by Bründlmayer, Prager, or Nigl.

sopas y ensaladas
soups and salads

sopa de lentejas
lentil soup

Lentil soup can be a little boring, but not this version, topped with smoky bacon, sharp cheese, and hot toasted chiles. But the real surprise is a garnish of grilled pineapple, whose tart yet sweet flavor profile brightens the soup considerably. Lentils are a great choice when you want a legume soup, because they cook up relatively quickly. Use regular brown lentils and the soup will be just fine. But for an extra-special lentil soup, make the soup with tiny French dark green *lentilles de Puy*, which can often be found at specialty grocery and natural-foods stores. MAKES 6 SERVINGS

Two ½-inch-thick slices peeled fresh pineapple

12 cups water

1¾ cups lentils, rinsed and picked over

1½ teaspoons fine sea salt, plus more to taste

1 pound ripe plum (Roma) tomatoes, cut into quarters

¼ red onion, coarsely chopped

2 garlic cloves, crushed

1 tablespoon canola oil

1 cup (4 ounces) grated queso añejo or romano cheese

6 slices bacon, cooked until crisp and crumbled

2 pasilla chiles, seeded, deveined, lightly toasted (see page 22), and crumbled

1. Prepare a hot fire in a charcoal grill or preheat a gas grill to high. Lightly oil the grill grids. Place the pineapple on the grill and cook, turning once, until heated through and seared on both sides with grill marks, about 5 minutes. Transfer to a cutting board, let cool, and chop coarsely, discarding the central core. Set aside at room temperature for up to 2 hours.

2. Bring 8 cups of the water to a boil in a large saucepan over high heat. Add the lentils and the 1½ teaspoons salt and return to a boil. Reduce the heat to medium-low and simmer until the lentils are tender, about 30 minutes. In batches, purée the lentils with their liquid in a blender, being sure to leave the lid slightly ajar to allow the steam to escape, and adding a bit more water if the purée is too thick. Transfer to a bowl. Rinse and dry the saucepan.

3. Meanwhile, bring the remaining 4 cups water and the tomatoes to a boil in a medium saucepan over high heat. Once the water boils, reduce the heat to medium and cook until the tomatoes collapse, about 10 minutes. Remove from the heat and let cool. In the blender, purée the tomatoes and their liquid with the onion and garlic. Strain through a sieve into a bowl to remove any stray seeds.

4. Heat the oil in the large saucepan over medium heat until it shimmers. Add the tomato mixture (it will splatter, so stand back) and bring to a boil. Reduce the heat to medium-low and simmer, stirring often, until slightly thickened. Add the lentil purée, increase the heat to high, and bring to a boil. Reduce the heat to medium and cook at a brisk simmer for 5 minutes. Season with salt.

5. To serve, ladle the soup into bowls and serve hot, topped with the pineapple, cheese, crumbled bacon, and chiles.

WINE NOTES
The earthiness of the lentils and the smokiness of the bacon are well complemented by an earthy Rioja such as Viña Ardanza, from La Rioja Alta.

gazpacho mexicano con nieve de pepino y serrano
mexican-style gazpacho with spicy cucumber sorbet

Gazpacho is, of course, a Spanish dish, and it can be quite mild. I much prefer it à la Mexicana, with the added zip of poblano chile. Wait until local tomatoes are in season before making this soup—it just isn't worth it with bland supermarket tomatoes that are shipped in from who-knows-where. And please remember that gazpacho should always be served ice-cold. The cucumber sorbet not only keeps the soup cold, but also imparts its own flavor as it melts. MAKES 6 SERVINGS

SPICY CUCUMBER SORBET

2 large cucumbers (1¼ pounds), peeled and seeded

1 serrano chile, seeded, deveined, and minced

1½ teaspoons fine sea salt

½ cup water

GAZPACHO

4 ripe red tomatoes (19 ounces total)

1 ripe yellow tomato

8 ounces seedless cucumber, thickly sliced

1 poblano chile, roasted, peeled (see page 22), and coarsely chopped

1½ cups water

1 tablespoon extra-virgin olive oil

Fine sea salt

1. To make the sorbet: Purée the cucumber, serrano chiles, salt, and water in a blender. Transfer the purée to a bowl, cover, and refrigerate until chilled, about 2 hours. Freeze in an ice cream maker according to the manufacturer's instructions. Transfer to an airtight container and freeze for at least 4 hours or up to 24 hours.

2. To make the gazpacho: Bring a medium saucepan of water to a boil over high heat. Add the red and yellow tomatoes to the water and cook until the skins loosen, about 30 seconds. Using a slotted spoon, transfer the tomatoes to a bowl of ice water. Peel the tomatoes. If the skins are stubborn, return the tomatoes to the boiling water until they loosen. Cut each tomato in half through its equator and poke out the seeds with your finger. Cut 1 red tomato and the yellow tomato into ¼-inch dice. Transfer to a bowl, cover, and refrigerate until ready to serve.

3. Purée the remaining tomatoes, cucumber, poblano chile, and water in a blender. Add the oil and season with salt to taste. Transfer to a bowl, cover, and refrigerate until ice-cold, at least 4 hours.

4. To serve, place a scoop of the cucumber sorbet in the center of each of 6 shallow soup bowls and sprinkle the chopped tomatoes around the sorbet. Ladle in the soup and serve immediately.

WINE NOTES

The flavors of the Mediterranean permeate this great summertime soup. A crisp, fruity rosé from Spain works well here. Good Spanish versions are made by Marqués de Riscal and Muga, both from Rioja.

sopa fría de aguacate y jaiba
chilled avocado and crab soup

This chilled soup is not only refreshing, but relatively substantial, thanks to the richness of the avocados and crab. Serve it for lunch on a hot summer's day, or as the first course of a meal with simply grilled meat as the entrée. MAKES 6 SERVINGS

5 cups water

1 celery rib, leaves removed, coarsely chopped

1 small leek, white and pale green parts only, coarsely chopped and well rinsed

1 garlic clove, crushed

2 ripe avocados, peeled, pitted, and coarsely chopped

4 cups whole milk

2 tablespoons fresh lime juice

Fine sea salt and freshly ground white pepper

9 ounces fresh lump crabmeat, picked over for shell

2 canned chipotles in adobo, thinly sliced

1. Bring 4 cups of the water, the celery, leek, and garlic to a boil in a medium saucepan over high heat. Reduce the heat to medium-low, cover, and cook until the vegetables are very soft, about 20 minutes. Purée the vegetables and their water in a blender with the remaining 1 cup water. Strain through a sieve into a bowl.

2. Purée the avocados and 2 cups of the milk in the blender; add the remaining 2 cups milk and blend on low speed until smooth. Transfer to a bowl and whisk in the vegetable mixture. Whisk in the lime juice and season to taste with salt and pepper. Transfer to a bowl, cover, and refrigerate until chilled, at least 4 hours.

3. To serve, divide equal amounts of the crab among 6 shallow soup bowls. Ladle in the soup, then garnish with the chipotle strips. Serve immediately.

WINE NOTES
The spice levels of this rich soup are low, so a rich, buttery Chardonnay would be fine; try Chateau St. Jean, Ferrari-Carano, or St. Francis, all from California.

sopa de elote y anís
corn soup with star anise

This soup celebrates corn in an elemental way. In fact, it's nothing more than corn, onion, salt, and water (not broth), splashed with a serrano chile drizzle. The warm flavors of star anise blend beautifully with the chile to create a distinctive seasoning. Because it is so bare-bones, reserve this recipe for when you get right-from-the-stalk corn at a farmers' market or roadside stand. Do not even consider making it with frozen or canned corn! MAKES 4 TO 6 SERVINGS

SOUP

8 ears corn

½ white onion, coarsely chopped

1½ teaspoons fine sea salt

5 cups water

CHILE–STAR ANISE DRIZZLE

½ cup water

4 serrano chiles, coarsely chopped (remove the seeds and veins if you want a milder flavor)

2 star anise pods, ground to a powder in a spice grinder (1 teaspoon)

⅛ teaspoon fine sea salt

1. To make the soup: Cut the corn kernels from the ears with a sharp knife. You should have about 4 cups. Working over a bowl, scrape the cobs with the knife to remove the "milk" from the cobs.

2. Bring the corn kernels, onion, salt, and water to a boil in a large saucepan over high heat. Reduce the heat to medium-low and simmer until the corn is tender, about 5 minutes. In batches, purée the corn mixture in a blender. Strain through a sieve into a bowl. Discard the solids. (The soup can be made up to 8 hours ahead and stored at room temperature. Just before serving, blend it again to recombine.)

3. To make the drizzle: Bring the water to a boil in a small saucepan over high heat. Add the chiles. Reduce the heat to medium-low and simmer until the chiles are soft, about 3 minutes. Transfer to a bowl and stir in the star anise and salt. (The drizzle can be made up to 5 days ahead, covered tightly and refrigerated.) Funnel into a plastic squeeze bottle for easy serving.

4. To serve, reheat the soup in a saucepan over low heat. Serve in shallow soup bowls, topped with a few drops of the chile drizzle. (Any leftover drizzle can be used as a hot sauce for meat, especially pork.)

WINE NOTES

Corn and Chardonnay have a natural affinity for each other. Because of the spiciness of the chile drizzle, it is best to have a rich-style wine with restrained oak such as Rosemount Diamond Label and Penfolds Koonunga Hill from Australia. For Californian wines, check out Beringer Founders Reserve or St. Francis.

ensalada de pulpo
grilled octopus salad

Unlike large octopus, which takes hours to cook, baby octopus simmers to tenderness in a relatively short period. Look for it at fishmongers that cater to restaurants or an Italian clientele. Mixed with a colorful cache of vegetables, this is a wonderful salad to savor. It is at its best when served at cool room temperature, not ice-cold. MAKES 6 SERVINGS

1 pound baby octopus

1 pound fava beans, shelled (1 cup)

1 ear of corn, kernels cut off (½ cup)

12 grape tomatoes, halved

1 poblano chile, roasted, peeled (see page 22), and cut into ¼-inch-wide strips

1 jalapeño chile, roasted, peeled (see page 22), and cut into ¼-inch-wide strips (optional)

LIME-OREGANO DRESSING

2 tablespoons fresh lime juice

1 tablespoon dried oregano, preferably Mexican

½ teaspoon fine sea salt

¼ teaspoon freshly ground black pepper

⅓ cup extra-virgin olive oil

1. Bring a large saucepan of salted water to a boil over high heat. Add the octopus and reduce the heat to medium. Cook at a brisk simmer until tender, about 10 minutes. Drain and rinse under cold water until cool enough to handle. Pull off the head and any viscera. Cut the tentacles into 2-inch lengths and place in a bowl.

2. Bring a medium saucepan of lightly salted water to a boil over high heat. Add the fava beans and cook until tender, about 5 minutes. Drain and rinse under cold water until cool enough to handle. Peel the fava beans. Add to the octopus.

3. Heat a heavy, medium skillet, preferably cast iron, over high heat. Add the corn kernels and cook, stirring occasionally, until lightly toasted, about 3 minutes. Add corn to bowl with the octopus and fava beans. Add the tomatoes, poblano, and jalapeño, if using. (The salad can be made up to 2 hours ahead, covered and refrigerated. Remove from the refrigerator 30 minutes before serving.)

4. To make the dressing: Whisk the lime juice, oregano, salt, and pepper in a small bowl. Gradually whisk in the oil. (The dressing can be made up to 2 hours ahead and kept at room temperature.)

5. Just before serving, pour the dressing over the salad and toss. Serve immediately.

WINE NOTES

Dry rosés work well with the octopus and cut the spiciness of the chiles. Good Spanish versions are made by Marqués de Riscal from Rioja. Excellent California examples are made by Joseph Phelps and Bonny Doon.

ensalada de verdolagas
purslane salad

Purslane isn't found at every produce market, but I bet you have some growing in your own garden, as it's a very prolific summertime weed. (Remember, many people love dandelion leaves, too.) When you do find this crisp, tart, succulentlike green at a farmers' market, use it in this salad, which has many different textures and flavors and is a pleasure to eat. It is one of my favorite greens, and I urge you to try this salad.   MAKES 4 SERVINGS

¼ cup pine nuts, toasted
(see page 26)

2 cups packed very coarsely
chopped purslane

12 grape tomatoes, halved

1 serrano chile, seeded,
deveined, and finely chopped

¼ cup grated queso fresco or
ricotta salata cheese

VINAIGRETTE

1½ tablespoons fresh
lime juice

Fine sea salt and freshly ground
black pepper

¼ cup extra-virgin olive oil

½ ripe avocado, peeled, pitted,
and thinly sliced

1. Toss the pine nuts, purslane, tomatoes, chile, and queso fresco in a large bowl.

2. To make the vinaigrette: Whisk the lime juice and salt and pepper to taste in a small bowl. Gradually whisk in the oil.

3. Just before serving, pour the vinaigrette over the salad and mix. Season the salad with salt and pepper. Divide among 4 salad plates, top with the sliced avocado, and serve immediately.

WINE NOTES
The earthiness of the purslane is complemented by Rieslings from Alsace such as those produced by Léon Beyer, Marcel Deiss, and Josmeyer. Sauvignon Blanc would also work well here. Try one from California's Frog's Leap or Duckhorn, or a Sancerre from the Loire Valley produced by Pascal Jolivet or Lucien Crochet.

ensalada de espinaca con aderezo de chipotle y miel
spinach salad with chipotle-honey dressing

The flavor of raw spinach, with a slight mineral edge, is balanced by sweet ingredients like caramelized onions and honey. Reserve the leftover dressing to serve as your house vinaigrette, as it is also delicious on other greens. MAKES 6 SERVINGS

CARAMELIZED ONIONS

1 tablespoon olive oil

1½ red onions, cut into thin half-moons

CHIPOTLE-HONEY DRESSING

¼ cup balsamic vinegar

¼ cup honey

2 canned chipotles in adobo plus more to taste

1 tablespoon Dijon mustard

¾ cup extra-virgin olive oil

8 cups baby spinach, rinsed and dried

1¼ cups (5 ounces) crumbled fresh goat cheese

4 tablespoons sesame seeds, toasted (see page 26)

Fine sea salt

1. To caramelize the onions: Heat the oil in a medium nonstick skillet over medium heat. Add the onions and reduce the heat to medium-low. Cook, stirring often, until tender, golden brown, and sweet, about 20 minutes. Let cool completely. (The onions can be prepared up to 1 day ahead, covered and refrigerated.)

2. To make the dressing: Pulse the vinegar, honey, chiles, and mustard in a blender or food processor. With the machine running, add the oil. (The dressing can be made up to 3 days ahead, covered and refrigerated. Whisk before using.)

3. Just before serving, toss the spinach, caramelized onions, goat cheese, and 3 tablespoons of the sesame seeds in a large bowl. Add ¼ cup of the dressing and toss again, adding more dressing, if you wish. Season with salt to taste. Divide among 6 salad plates, sprinkle with the remaining 1 tablespoon sesame seeds, and serve immediately. Save remaining dressing for another use.

WINE NOTES

Though Sauvignon Blanc is great with goat cheese, this salad has a good amount of sweetness due to the caramelized onions and the honey in the dressing. A good match is a Kabinett-level German Riesling, in particular the Robert Weil Riesling from the Rheingau.

ensalada de nopales
cactus salad

Do not be afraid of this salad. Nopales (cactus leaves) are quite delicious and may remind you of green beans or okra. In fact, you could make this salad with green beans perfectly well. But do try the nopales if you never have—you may discover a new favorite vegetable. You will find canned nopales at Latino markets, but fresh ones are much better. **MAKES 6 SERVINGS**

NOPALES

6 nopales (cactus leaves)

1 onion, quartered

4 garlic cloves, crushed

DRESSING

¼ cup cider vinegar

1 tablespoon dried oregano, preferably Mexican

1 tablespoon red pepper flakes

¾ cup extra-virgin olive oil

Fine sea salt

3 plum (Roma) tomatoes, cut into thin wedges

½ red onion, thinly sliced

½ cup chopped fresh cilantro

1 avocado, peeled, pitted, and thinly sliced

½ cup (2 ounces) shredded queso fresco or ricotta salata cheese

1. To prepare the nopales: If necessary, use a small sharp knife to remove any residual thorns or nodules from the cactus leaves. Bring 8 cups salted water to a boil in a large saucepan over high heat. Add the nopales, onion, and garlic and reduce the heat to medium. Cook at a brisk simmer until the nopales are tender, about 6 minutes. Drain and rinse under cold water. Discard the onion and garlic. Cut the nopales into strips about ½ inch wide and 2½ inches long. Cover and refrigerate until chilled, at least 2 hours or up to 2 days.

2. To make the dressing: Whisk the vinegar, oregano, and red pepper flakes in a small bowl. Gradually whisk in the oil. Season with salt to taste.

3. Mix the nopales, tomatoes, red onion, and cilantro in a medium bowl. Add as much dressing as you like (refrigerate any remaining dressing for another use) and toss. Divide the salad among 6 salad plates and top with the avocado and queso fresco. Serve immediately.

WINE NOTES

The vinaigrette in this salad can be overpowered by most wines, but an Alsatian Gewürztraminer will hold its ground. Producers to look for are Zind-Humbrecht, Hugel, Weinbach, and Domaine Ostertag.

ensalada de nochebuena
christmas eve salad

In many parts of Mexico, *ensalada de nochebuena* is as traditional at Christmas as candy canes are in America. While you will find other recipes that include bananas, pomegranate seeds, carrots, and mayonnaise, my version is streamlined to showcase my preferred ingredients. It is usually served from a big bowl, but I love how it looks individually plated. You'll need a star-shaped cookie cutter to cut the beets. MAKES 8 SERVINGS

4 beets

1 jícama (1¼ pounds)

⅓ cup fresh orange juice

Fine sea salt

⅓ cup extra-virgin olive oil

2 navel oranges, peeled and segmented (see Note)

½ cup roasted peanuts, coarsely chopped

1 tablespoon pure ground chile, preferably pequín

1. To roast the beets: Position a rack in the center of the oven and preheat the oven to 400°F. If the greens are attached to the beets, cut them off, leaving ½ inch of the stems intact. Scrub the beets well under cold water. Wrap each beet in aluminum foil and place on a baking sheet. Bake until tender when pierced with a metal skewer (test right through the foil), about 1 hour, depending on the age of the beets. Unwrap them and let cool until easy to handle but still warm. Peel the beets. Cut each beet crosswise into 6 slices. Cut each slice into a star with a star-shaped cookie cutter. Transfer the beet stars to a plate, cover, and refrigerate until ready to serve. (The beets can be prepared up to 12 hours ahead.)

2. Using a sturdy vegetable peeler or a paring knife, peel the jícama. Cut it into ¼-by-2-inch strips. Transfer to a bowl, cover, and refrigerate until ready to serve. (The jícama can be prepared up to 2 hours ahead of serving.)

3. Whisk the orange juice and salt to taste in a small bowl. Gradually whisk in the oil.

4. Divide the jícama among 8 salad plates. Top each with 3 beet stars and 3 orange segments, then a scattering of peanuts. Drizzle the orange-juice dressing over the salads, then dust the entire plate with the ground chile. Serve immediately.

NOTE: To peel and segment citrus, trim the top and bottom off a citrus fruit so it stands on the work counter. Using a serrated knife, cut off the thick peel where it meets the flesh to end up with a skinless sphere. Working over a medium bowl to catch the juices, hold the fruit in one hand, and cut between the thin membranes to release the segments into the bowl. Cover and refrigerate for up to 1 day. Drain the segments before using.

WINE NOTES
This salad is well paired with a California Viognier. Look for one produced by Terre Rouge, Alban, Calera, or Arrowood.

mariscos
seafood entrées

pescado al tequila
halibut in parchment with tequila

When ingredients are enclosed in a parchment paper packet and cooked, the ensuing juices are trapped and concentrated. Usually the packets are baked, but steaming is a gentle way of cooking, especially successful with delicate ingredients like fish. Here I've combined the somewhat meaty flavor and texture of halibut and shiitake mushrooms with smooth tequila. You will need a large steamer with three stacked racks to efficiently hold the four packets. Reasonably priced aluminum models are available at Asian markets. Allow guests to open their packets at the table so they can fully appreciate the heady aroma as it is released. This dish is great served with Rice with Poblano Chiles (page 150) MAKES 4 SERVINGS

3 tablespoons olive oil

1 small white onion, finely chopped

2 serrano chiles, seeded, deveined, and minced

12 ounces shiitakes, stemmed and sliced

3 garlic cloves, minced

About ½ cup silver tequila, preferably 100% agave

About ⅓ cup chopped fresh cilantro

Fine sea salt and freshly ground black pepper

Four 6- to 7-ounce halibut fillets

1. Heat the oil in a large skillet over medium-high heat. Add the onion and chiles and cook, stirring often, until the onion softens, about 4 minutes. Add the mushrooms and cook, stirring often, until they are tender, about 4 minutes more. Add the garlic and cook, stirring often, until it gives off its aroma, about 1 minute. Add ⅓ cup of the tequila. Using a long match and averting your face, ignite the tequila and let it burn until the flames go out. Remove from the heat and stir in the cilantro. Season with salt and pepper to taste.

2. Have ready four 12-inch square sheets of parchment paper. Fold 1 square in half and open. Place 1 fillet on the parchment square below the fold and season lightly with salt and pepper. Place one-fourth of the mushroom mixture on top and sprinkle with about 2 teaspoons of the remaining tequila. Fold the square over and crimp the 3 open edges closed to tightly seal the packet. Repeat with the remaining squares and ingredients. (The packets can be prepared up to 2 hours ahead and refrigerated. Remove from the refrigerator 30 minutes before steaming.)

3. Prepare an aluminum stacked steamer: Fill the bottom of the steamer with about 1 inch of water and bring to a boil over high heat. Leaving the bottom rack empty (if the packets are too close to the steam, they will cook unevenly), arrange 2 packets in each rack, stack the racks, and cover tightly with the lid. Boil over high heat with a full head of steam for about 15 minutes.

4. Transfer each packet to a dinner plate and serve, allowing each guest to open the packet at the table. Provide each guest with a sharp-tipped knife to pierce the paper, or pass scissors.

WINE NOTES
Sauvignon Blanc is a nice complement to this dish's herbal notes. Fine examples from France are Sancerre by Pascal Jolivet or Lucien Crochet, or Pouilly-Fumé from Michel Redde et Fils or Ladoucette. From New Zealand, look for Villa Maria or Brancott.

salmón con salsa de papaya roja y tequila
salmon with red papaya–tequila sauce

Salmon is such a versatile fish that it goes well even with sweet flavors, like this fruity red sauce the color of a Pacific sunset. Red papaya (also called Mexican papaya) not only has a more intense color than the golden variety, its flavor and size are pumped up a bit as well. You will find it during its springtime season at Latino markets and well-stocked produce stores, but if you can find only the familiar golden papaya, go ahead and use it. The dish also includes a grapefruit and corn salsa, a wonderful sweet and savory combination enhanced by a coarse salt such as *fleur de sel*. MAKES 6 SERVINGS

RED PAPAYA–TEQUILA SAUCE

1 pound ripe red papaya, peeled, seeded, and chopped (about 3 cups)

⅓ cup plus 1 tablespoon high-quality silver tequila

2 tablespoons fresh lime juice

GRAPEFRUIT-CORN SALSA

2 ears corn, kernels cut off (1 cup)

1 pink grapefruit, peeled and segmented (see page 90)

1 ripe avocado, peeled, pitted, and cut into ½-inch dice

¼ cup fresh cilantro leaves

3 scallions, white part only, thinly sliced

3 fresh chiles de árbol or 1 serrano chile, seeded, deveined, and minced

2 tablespoons fresh lime juice

1½ tablespoons extra-virgin olive oil

Six 6- to 7-ounce salmon fillets, preferable sockeye

Olive oil for brushing

Fine sea salt and freshly ground black pepper

½ cup Four-Chile Sauce (page 166)

3 radishes, very thinly sliced, for garnish

Fleur de sel, sel de Guérande, or kosher salt

1. Prepare a hot fire in a charcoal grill, or preheat a gas grill to high.

2. To make the sauce: Purée the papaya, tequila, and lime juice in a blender until smooth. (The sauce can be made up to 1 day ahead, covered and refrigerated. Remove from the refrigerator 1 hour before serving.)

3. Heat a heavy medium skillet, preferably cast iron, over high heat. Add the corn kernels and cook, stirring occasionally, until lightly toasted, about 3 minutes. Let cool.

4. To make the salsa: Combine the grapefruit, cooled corn, avocado, cilantro, scallions, chiles, lime juice, and oil in a medium bowl. Set aside.

(The salsa can be made up to 2 hours ahead, covered and stored at room temperature.)

5. Lightly brush the salmon on both sides with the oil and season to taste with salt and pepper. Lightly oil the grill grids. Cook the salmon until seared with grill marks on the bottom, about 2 minutes. Turn and cook until grill-marked on the other side and still slightly translucent in the center, about 2 minutes more. Do not overcook the salmon. Transfer to a platter.

6. For each serving, spread about ⅓ cup Red Papaya–Tequila Sauce in the center of a dinner plate. Top with a salmon fillet and about ½ cup of the Grapefruit-Corn Salsa. Drizzle 2 tablespoons of the Four-Chile Sauce around the plate and garnish with the sliced radishes. (You may have extra salsa, which you can serve in bowls alongside.) Sprinkle the salsa with salt. Serve immediately.

WINE NOTES
The richness of the salmon requires an equally rich, yet not heavily oaked wine. Try an Alsatian Gewürztraminer (Zind-Humbrecht, Weinbach, or Hugel) or a California Viognier (Miner, Alban, or Terre Rouge).

salmón al hinojo glaseado con chile ancho
ancho-glazed salmon with fennel

Salmon can stand up to many different flavors, but that doesn't mean it's a bully in the kitchen, overpowering everything it comes into contact with. In this dish, it matches up with quite a few ingredients, from tomatillos to ancho chiles, and does so well. This recipe is perfect for an autumn dinner, as it includes three cold-weather vegetables: fennel, red Swiss chard, and beets. Cooking the salmon on an outdoor grill adds a nice smoky layer of flavor, but it can be broiled. MAKES 4 SERVINGS

1 small bulb fennel, trimmed and cored (reserve fronds)

2 tablespoons olive oil plus more for brushing

6 cups baby red Swiss chard or baby spinach

Fine sea salt and freshly ground black pepper

1 cup Roasted Tomatillo Sauce (page 165)

¾ cup heavy cream

Four 7-ounce salmon fillets, preferably wild, skinned, pin bones removed

1 cup Ancho–Honey Sauce (page 166)

1 red beet, roasted, peeled (see page 90), and cut into ¼-inch dice

1. Prepare a medium-hot fire in a charcoal grill, or preheat a gas grill to medium-hot.

2. Cut the fennel bulb in half lengthwise, thinly slice the fennel halves crosswise. Heat 1 tablespoon of the oil in a large skillet over medium-high heat and add the fennel. Cook, stirring occasionally, until crisp-tender, about 5 minutes. Using a slotted spoon, transfer to a bowl.

3. Heat the remaining 1 tablespoon oil in the skillet over medium-high heat. Add the Swiss chard and cook, stirring occasionally, until slightly wilted, about 2 minutes. Stir in the fennel. Season to taste with salt and pepper. Set aside and keep warm.

4. Bring the Roasted Tomatillo Sauce and heavy cream to a boil in a medium saucepan over high heat, stirring often and taking care that the mixture doesn't boil over. Reduce the heat to medium and cook at a brisk simmer until slightly reduced, about 5 minutes. Set aside and keep warm.

5. Preheat the broiler to high. Brush the salmon on both sides with olive oil and season to taste with salt and pepper. Scrub the grill grids as clean as possible with a grill brush and oil the grids (this helps to keep the fish from sticking). Place the salmon, skinned side up, on the grill. Cook until grill-marked on the bottom, about 3 minutes.

Turn the salmon and cook until grill-marked on the other side and still slightly translucent in the center, about 4 minutes more. Brush the Ancho-Honey Sauce over the fillets and place under the hot broiler for 30 seconds for the sauce to glaze.

6. Heap an equal amount of the chard mixture in the center of each of 4 dinner plates. Place the salmon on top, then spoon the tomatillo-cream sauce around the chard. Garnish with the diced beet and reserved fennel fronds. Serve immediately.

WINE NOTES
Salmon is one fish that goes well with red wine, specifically Pinot Noir, with its silken texture and taste. Ripe yet lightly oaked examples work best. Excellent producers from California are Au Bon Climat, Tudor, Saintsbury, and Littorai. From Oregon, look for Argyle, Ken Wright, or Ponzi.

pescado con hongos y dos salsas
black sea bass with mushrooms and two sauces

You will discover many pleasures in every bite of this dish: mushrooms that have been mildly heated by chile veins, herbaceous epazote, a sweet Mango Sauce, a complex Four-Chile Sauce, and smooth Potato Cakes with Aged Mexican Cheese, all combined with firm-fleshed sea bass. The various components can all be prepared ahead of time, with just a final sauté of the fish and the potato cakes. MAKES 4 SERVINGS

MUSHROOM SAUCE

3 tablespoons olive oil

½ cup chopped white onion

6 garlic cloves, minced

12 veins from dried chiles, such as anchos, pasillas, or guajillos (see Note)

1 pound shiitakes, stemmed and sliced

½ cup chopped fresh epazote, or ¼ cup chopped fresh oregano

Fine sea salt

3 tablespoons olive oil

Four 6- to 7-ounce black sea bass fillets, skinned

Fine sea salt and freshly ground black pepper

Potato Cakes with Aged Mexican Cheese (page 146) for serving

1 cup Mango Sauce (page 171) in a squeeze bottle

1 cup Four-Chile Sauce (page 166) in a squeeze bottle

1. To make the Mushroom Sauce: Heat the oil in a large skillet over medium-high heat. Add the onion and cook until it begins to soften, about 2 minutes. Stir in the garlic and chile veins and cook, uncovered, until the garlic is fragrant, about 1 minute. Stir in the mushrooms, cover, and reduce the heat to low. Cook, stirring occasionally, until the mushrooms give off their juices, about 3 minutes. Remove from the heat and stir in the epazote. Season to taste with salt. (The Mushroom Sauce can be prepared up to 2 hours ahead and kept at room temperature. Reheat before serving.)

2. Heat the oil in a very large nonstick skillet over medium-high heat until shimmering. Pat the fish dry with paper towels and season to taste with salt and pepper. Add the fish to the skillet and cook until golden on the bottom, about 3 minutes. Turn and cook just until barely opaque throughout, about 2 minutes longer. Transfer the fish to a platter.

3. For each serving, place 2 potato cakes on a dinner plate, top with the fish, then one-fourth of the mushroom mixture. Squeeze a circle of Mango Sauce around the fish, then a concentric circle of Four-Chile Sauce outside of the Mango Sauce. Serve immediately.

NOTE: The seeds and veins are often removed from chiles before using because they contain the highest concentration of capsaicin, the component that is responsible for the heat. Their removal gives the cook better control over the spiciness of the finished dish. That does not mean that the seeds and veins are unusable. In fact, the veins are much more delicate in texture than the chile flesh and can be used as a seasoning. (As for the seeds, if you want to pump up the heat of a dish, just sprinkle in a few.) At ¡Salpicón! we have a constant supply of chile veins, but if you don't, you have two options. Looking ahead to when you might need the veins, as you clean chiles over the course of time, collect the veins in an airtight container and store in a cool, dry place. Or cut an ancho, pasilla, or guajillo chile into very thin threads and soak them in hot water until softened, about 5 minutes. Drain the chile threads and pat dry with paper towels before using.

WINE NOTES

This dish combines the tropical flavors of the Mango Sauce with the spicy notes of the Four-Chile Sauce, and Gewürztraminer pairs well with both. Try bottlings by Zind-Humbrecht, Weinbach, Hugel, or Léon Beyer.

pescado a la veracruzana
fish fillets veracruz-style

Veracruz is well known for this intriguingly seasoned fish in tomato sauce. The sauce is always studded
with olives and capers, ingredients that reflect the Spanish influence on the culture and cuisine of this port city.
But it is the Mexican touches of cinnamon, cloves, and pickled jalapeño that supply the real character.
This wonderful dish is one of the easiest, lightest, and most delicious of all of Mexico's culinary treasures.
Use any firm, white-fleshed fish (I've listed my favorites below) and adjust the simmering time as required by
its thickness—the fish should be just opaque throughout. MAKES 6 SERVINGS

VERACRUZ TOMATO SAUCE

3 tablespoons extra-virgin
olive oil

1 small onion, thinly sliced

3 garlic cloves, minced

2 pounds ripe plum (Roma)
tomatoes, roasted (see page 26),
peeled, seeded, and chopped

25 manzanilla or other green
olives, pitted and halved (about
½ cup)

⅓ cup nonpareil capers, drained

2 pickled jalapeños (page 25), or
use bottled

2 teaspoons finely chopped
fresh thyme

½ teaspoon ground cinnamon

Pinch of ground cloves

½ cup finely chopped fresh
flat-leaf parsley

Fine sea salt

¼ cup extra-virgin olive oil

Six 6-ounce fish fillets, such as
red snapper, mahi mahi,
or grouper

Fine sea salt and freshly ground
black pepper

1. To make the sauce: Heat the oil in a large skillet
over medium heat. Add the onion and cook, stirring
occasionally, until translucent, about 3 minutes.
Add the garlic and cook until golden and fragrant,
about 2 minutes more. Stir in the tomatoes, cover,
and cook until they give off their juices, about
6 minutes. Stir in the olives, capers, jalapeños,
thyme, cinnamon, and cloves. Cook until the olives
are heated through, about 2 minutes. Stir in the
parsley and season to taste with salt. (The sauce
can be cooled, covered, and refrigerated for up
to 24 hours. Reheat before using.) Set aside and
keep warm.

2. Heat the oil in a large nonstick skillet over
medium-high heat. Pat the fish dry with paper
towels and season to taste with salt and pepper.
Place in the skillet and cook until golden on the
bottom, about 3 minutes. (Do not disturb the fish
unnecessarily—allow it to develop a bottom crust
and it will be easier to turn without sticking.) Turn
the fish and add the warm tomato sauce. Bring to
a simmer, cover, and cook until the fish is opaque
throughout, 3 to 4 minutes longer.

3. To serve, use a slotted spatula to transfer each
fillet to a dinner plate. Spoon the tomato sauce on
top and serve hot.

WINE NOTES
This Mediterranean-style sauce would be
perfect with a Spanish Albariño (Martín Códax
or Pazo de Señoráns) or a Portuguese Vinho
Verde Alvarinho by Casal Mendes or Aveleda.

pescado alcaparrado con chilacas rellenas
fish in caper sauce with stuffed chilaca chiles

By "caper sauce," I don't mean the typical butter sauce with capers, but a thick green sauce of capers puréed with roasted tomatillos. The raisin garnish adds a touch of sweetness that balances the pleasant bitterness of the capers, so don't skip it. And the fresh chiles are a very simple but interesting and professional-looking garnish. If you can't find chilaca chiles, use another moderately hot variety, such as Anaheim. MAKES 4 SERVINGS

STUFFED CHILACA CHILES

4 chilaca chiles or other long green chiles

¼ cup fresh goat cheese at room temperature

2 tablespoons pine nuts, toasted (see page 25)

Pinch of fine sea salt

1 cup Roasted Tomatillo Sauce (page 165)

⅓ cup capers, drained and rinsed

2 tablespoons extra-virgin olive oil

½ cup all-purpose flour

Salt and freshly ground black pepper

Four 6- to 7-ounce firm-fleshed white fish fillets, such as mahi mahi, grouper, sea bass, or red snapper

⅓ cup raisins for garnish

1. To make the chiles: Position the broiler rack about 6 inches from the heat source and preheat the broiler. Broil the chiles, turning occasionally, until the skin is blistered but not blackened, about 8 minutes. (The idea here is to loosen the skin enough to remove it, but to keep the chile flesh relatively firm so the chile will keep its shape.) Transfer to a plate and cover with aluminum foil. Let stand for about 3 minutes. Remove the skin. Make a lengthwise incision in each chile and carefully remove the seeds and veins, keeping the chile otherwise intact.

2. Mix the goat cheese, pine nuts, and salt in a small bowl. Use a spoon to stuff each chile with an equal amount of the mixture. Cover and let stand at room temperature for up to 2 hours.

3. Purée the Roasted Tomatillo Sauce and capers together in a blender. Transfer to a small saucepan and bring to a simmer. Set aside and keep warm.

4. Heat the oil in a large skillet over medium-high heat. Season the flour to taste with salt and pepper and spread on a plate. Dredge the fish fillets in the flour mixture and shake off the excess. Place in the skillet and cook until golden on the bottom, about 3 minutes. Turn the fish and cook until golden on the other side, about 3 minutes longer.

5. Transfer each fish fillet to a dinner plate. Top each with tomatillo-caper sauce, and then sprinkle with raisins. Add a stuffed chile to each plate and serve at once.

WINE NOTES
The acidity in the caper sauce is well suited with an Albariño from Spain. Try one produced by Martín Códax, Lagar de Fornelos, or Pazo de Señoráns. Also excellent are dry rosés from Bandol in Provence made by Domaine Tempier and Domaines Ott.

jaibas al mojo de ajo
soft-shell crabs with sweet garlic sauce

From Memorial Day to Labor Day, soft-shell crabs are in season, and they should be savored as often as possible during this all-too-brief period. Fry them until they are nice and crispy, so the outside contrasts with the tender flesh. You'll need 2 large skillets for 8 crabs—do not crowd them while frying or they will steam and lose their crunchy texture. The garlic sauce (actually a *mojo*, which is more of a flavored oil) echoes the sweetness of the crabmeat. Note that the garlic cooks long and slow, so be patient. MAKES 4 SERVINGS

SWEET GARLIC SAUCE

30 large, plump garlic cloves (from about 3 heads), peeled

1 cup skim milk

1 cup extra-virgin olive oil

2 guajillo chiles, seeded, deveined, and coarsely chopped

¼ cup fresh lime juice

Fine sea salt

½ cup all-purpose flour

Fine sea salt and freshly ground black pepper

8 jumbo soft-shell crabs, cleaned (see Note)

1 cup olive oil

2 ripe avocados, peeled, pitted, and cut into ½-inch dice

1. To make the sauce: Bring the garlic cloves and skim milk to a boil in a small, heavy saucepan over medium heat, taking care that the milk doesn't boil over. Reduce the heat to low and simmer for 2 minutes. Drain, discarding the milk. Transfer the garlic to a food processor (preferably a mini–food processor) and pulse until minced.

2. Clean and dry the saucepan. Add the oil and heat over medium heat just until warm. Add the garlic and immediately reduce the heat to very low. If you have a heat diffuser, use it. Gently cook the garlic until it turns golden but not browned, 1½ to 2 hours. It is important that the oil heats at the lowest possible temperature, or the garlic will turn bitter. Remove from the heat and stir in the chiles and lime juice. Season to taste with salt. Set aside. (The sauce can be made up to 4 hours ahead and kept at room temperature. Reheat gently before serving.)

3. Spread the flour in a shallow dish and season to taste with salt and pepper. Dredge the crabs in the flour, shaking off the excess. Place the crabs on a waxed-paper-lined baking sheet.

4. Heat ½ cup oil in each of 2 large skillets over high heat until it shimmers. Add the crabs and cook until golden brown on the bottom, about 2 minutes. (Stand back, as the crabs can splatter.) Carefully turn the crabs and cook until crispy on the second side, about 2 minutes longer. Using a slotted metal spatula, transfer to paper towels to drain briefly.

5. Place 2 crabs on each dinner plate and spoon about 1 tablespoon of sauce over each crab. Garnish with the diced avocado and serve immediately.

NOTE: Have the fishmonger clean the crabs for you. The crabs should be cooked within 8 hours of cleaning.

WINE NOTES

The garlic sauce in this dish is not harsh but sweet, because it is cooked for a long time. The chiles are just an accent and are quite mild, so you're basically matching the sweet crab with a wine. In this case, I would choose a ripe-style, restrained-oak Chardonnay such as Chateau Montelena from California or Penfolds from Australia.

caldo de mariscos
seafood stew

One of the most simple and delicious of dinner entrées, this fragrant stew sports a generous variety of seafood swimming in a chile-infused fish stock. The different components should be added to the simmering stock in stages so they can reach their individual point of doneness. As it is done, transfer the seafood to a large serving bowl, and keep the bowl covered so the fish doesn't cool too much. When the seafood is served with the piping hot stock, it will come back up to temperature. The serving bowls should be warmed, too, so heat them gently in a preheated low oven for a few minutes. Or, if your china is delicate, fill each bowl with very hot water and let stand to heat the bowl, then pour out the water and dry the bowls. **MAKES 6 SERVINGS**

FISH STOCK

3 pounds bones from white-fleshed fish (not oily fish like salmon or mackerel)

1 gallon water

1 white onion, coarsely chopped

4 carrots, coarsely chopped

1 celery rib, coarsely chopped

7 garlic cloves, crushed

2 teaspoons fine sea salt

GUAJILLO CHILE SEASONING

15 dried guajillo chiles, seeded and deveined

¼ white onion, coarsely chopped

4 garlic cloves

About ½ cup Fish Stock (above)

Fine sea salt

18 clams, preferably Manila, scrubbed

12 mussels, preferably New Zealand, scrubbed

1 pound monkfish, cut into bite-size pieces

12 jumbo or extra-large shrimp, shelled and deveined

12 sea scallops, preferably dry packed (day-boat or diver) scallops

12 ounces calamari (squid), cleaned and cut crosswise into ¼-inch-thick rings

½ onion, finely chopped, for serving

2 tablespoons finely chopped fresh cilantro for serving

2 limes, cut into wedges, for serving

1. To make the stock: Put the fish bones in a colander and rinse under cold running water until the water runs clear. Put the bones in a stockpot with the water, onion, carrots, celery, garlic, and salt. Bring to a boil over high heat. Reduce the heat to medium-low and simmer until full flavored, about 45 minutes. Do not overcook or the stock will become bitter. Line a sieve with a moistened, wrung-out cheesecloth. Strain the stock through the sieve into a large bowl, discarding the solids. (Or, remove the meat from the fish bones to roll with warm corn tortillas and salsa for a fish taco snack.) Pour the stock into a medium saucepan and bring to a low simmer over low heat. Keep the stock hot.

2. To make the chile seasoning: Put the chiles in a medium bowl and add boiling water to cover. Let stand until the chiles are softened, about 20 minutes. Drain the chiles, discarding the soaking liquid, and transfer to a blender. Add the onion and garlic and purée with ½ cup stock or more as needed to make a thick sauce.

recipe continues

3. Pour the chile purée into the remaining stock and bring to a boil over high heat. Return the heat to medium-low and simmer for 15 minutes. (The stock can be made up to 1 day ahead, cooled, covered, and refrigerated. Reheat to a simmer before proceeding.) Season the stock to taste with salt and keep very hot.

4. Place a large serving bowl and a lid to cover the bowl (a pot lid works fine) near the stove. Transfer 3 cups of the stock to a large saucepan and bring to a boil over high heat. Add the clams, cover, and cook until the clams open, about 5 minutes. Discard any clams that do not open. Using a large wire-mesh skimmer, transfer the clams to the bowl and cover. Repeat with the mussels.

5. Add the monkfish to the stock and simmer just until it turns opaque, about 4 minutes. Transfer it to the bowl of shellfish. Add the shrimp to the stock and cook for 2 minutes, but do not remove. Add the scallops to the stock and cook for 2 minutes, then add the calamari and cook for 30 seconds, or until all the seafood is opaque. Using a wire-mesh skimmer, transfer them to the bowl of seafood.

6. To serve, bring the pot of hot stock and the bowl of seafood to the table. Divide the seafood among 6 warmed deep soup bowls. Add the piping hot stock, and accompany with bowls of onion, chopped cilantro, and lime wedges.

WINE NOTES

A dry Riesling from just about anywhere works fine here—Austrian, Alsatian, or Australian all go well with the fish and shellfish. A New World Pinot Noir with light oak also works very well. From California, look for Cosentino, Saintsbury, and Laetitia. Or, from Oregon, choose Domaine Serene, Panther Creek, or Ponzi.

mejillones al cilantro con vino blanco y chiles serranos
mussels with white wine, serranos, and cilantro

Cilantro and chiles perk up a classic dish of mussels steamed in white wine. Plenty of garlic bread for sopping up the juices is an essential part of the recipe. You may find two kinds of mussels at the market: wild and cultured. At ¡Salpicón!, we use the best mussels of the season, from Mediterranean to green lip, as the different varieties have seasons when they are at their best. MAKES 4 SERVINGS

GARLIC BREAD

1 loaf crusty country-style bread

8 tablespoons (1 stick) unsalted butter, at room temperature

8 garlic cloves, minced

½ cup finely chopped fresh flat-leaf parsley

Fine sea salt

3 tablespoons unsalted butter

1 tablespoon olive oil

1 white onion, finely chopped

2 serrano chiles, deveined, seeded, and minced

4 garlic cloves, minced

4 pounds wild or cultivated mussels (see Note)

½ cup dry white wine

½ cup finely chopped fresh cilantro

Fine sea salt

1. To make the garlic bread: Cut the bread into slices about ¾ inch thick. Mix the butter, garlic, and parsley in a small bowl and season to taste with salt. Spread the butter on each slice and re-form the loaf into its original shape. Wrap in aluminum foil. (The garlic bread can be made up to 8 hours ahead and stored at room temperature.)

2. Preheat the oven to 350°F. Bake the bread until it is heated through, about 30 minutes.

3. Melt the butter with the oil in a large saucepan over medium heat. Add the onion and chiles and cook, stirring often, until the onion softens, about 4 minutes. Add the garlic and cook until fragrant, about 2 minutes longer. Add the mussels, wine, and cilantro and bring the wine to a boil. Cover and cook until the mussels open, about 5 minutes. Season the cooking liquid with salt to taste, keeping in mind that mussels are naturally salty.

4. To serve, use tongs to divide the mussels among 4 large bowls. Ladle in equal amounts of the cooking liquid. Serve at once, with the hot bread passed on the side.

NOTE: To prepare wild mussels, use pliers to remove the small, tough cord of fibers (called a beard) near the pointed end of the shell. Soak the mussels in salted cold water for an hour or so, then drain and scrub them well. Cultured mussels, often labeled Prince Edward Island (or PEI) for the location of the most famous beds, do not need any special attention. In either case, discard any partially opened mussels that do not close when rapped, or any wild ones that feel heavy for their size (they could be filled with mud).

WINE NOTES

This dish is on the mild side, so any wine that complements shellfish is fine. Just about any Sauvignon Blanc from France, California, or New Zealand would be excellent. Also, try a dry Riesling from Austria, Alsace, or Australia.

ostiones con crema de chipotle
oysters in chipotle cream sauce

This is my interpretation of oysters Rockefeller—I love the creamy sauce combined with the briny shellfish. Use the best oysters in season you can find. You can open the oysters yourself, but it is much easier to have your fishmonger open them for you. Bring them home on a bed of ice and use them within a few hours of opening.

MAKES 4 FIRST-COURSE SERVINGS OR 2 ENTRÉE SERVINGS

½ cup heavy cream

2 canned chipotle chiles in adobo, or more to taste

Pinch of fine sea salt

24 oysters, scrubbed and opened (see Note)

48 baby spinach leaves

1 cup (4 ounces) shredded Chihuahua or Monterey Jack cheese

1. Crumple a couple of sheets of aluminum foil on a baking sheet. Purée the cream, chipotles, and salt in a blender. Spoon 1 teaspoon of the chile cream over each oyster. Top each with 2 spinach leaves and about 2 teaspoons of the cheese. Nestle the oysters in the foil to keep them level. (The oysters can be prepared 1 hour before serving and refrigerated.)

2. Position a broiler rack 6 to 8 inches from the heat source and preheat the broiler. If your broiler heat can be adjusted, set it for medium or low heat. The heat should be moderate so the oysters are just heated through by the time the cheese browns. Broil the oysters until the cheese is golden brown, about 5 minutes. Serve immediately.

NOTE: To open the oysters, supply yourself with an oyster knife and a pair of thick gloves (or protect your hand with a pot holder). Hold the oyster, rounded side down, in your hand. Find where the two shell halves meet, near the pointed end of the oyster. Wedge the tip of the oyster knife about ½ inch from the pointed end—this takes some determination. Push down on the knife handle to lever the knife and force the shells apart. Slide the knife along the flatter upper shell to release the top part of the meat. Remove the top shell. Slide the knife in the cupped bottom shell to fully detach the meat. Set aside on a piece of crumpled aluminum foil to keep the shell upright.

WINE NOTES
Although the sauce uses chipotle chiles, the cream tempers them, so a good match would be a ripe-style Chardonnay with restrained oak such as those made by Au Bon Climat or Cakebread.

carnes y aves
meat and poultry entrées

carne en mole verde
beef in green mole

This mole is from the central part of Mexico, where my mother was raised. Unlike dark moles, which are made with dried chiles, it is green with tomatillos, lettuce, pumpkin seeds, and green serrano chiles. I prefer cubes of beef brisket for this stew, but you could use beef chuck if brisket isn't available. Mexican Rice (page 153) makes a good accompaniment. MAKES 6 SERVINGS

2 pounds beef brisket, cut into 2-inch pieces

1 gallon water

1 onion, quartered

3 garlic cloves, crushed

1 tablespoon fine sea salt

GREEN MOLE

½ cup sesame seeds, toasted (see page 26)

½ cup shelled pumpkin seeds (pepitas), toasted (see page 26)

6 tomatillos, husked, rinsed, and coarsely chopped

6 outer romaine lettuce leaves, trimmed of white ribs and coarsely chopped

⅓ cup chopped white onion

2 serrano chiles, seeded, deveined, and minced

2 garlic cloves

1 teaspoon black peppercorns

4 cloves

2 cups beef broth from brisket, above

2 tablespoons canola oil

Fine sea salt

1. Bring the brisket, water, onion, garlic, and salt to a boil in a large stockpot over high heat. Reduce the heat to medium-low and simmer until the meat is tender, about 2½ hours. Drain in a sieve over a bowl; discard the onion and garlic and reserve the beef. Measure 2 cups of the broth and reserve the remaining broth for another use.

2. To make the mole: Combine the sesame seeds and pumpkin seeds, tomatillos, lettuce leaves, onion, chiles, garlic, peppercorns, and cloves in a large bowl. In batches, purée the mixture in a blender, adding the beef broth as needed to make a smooth sauce, and transfer to a bowl.

3. Heat the oil in a large saucepan over medium heat. Add the mole, being careful that it doesn't splatter. Reduce the heat to medium-low and simmer, stirring often, until nicely thickened, about 20 minutes. Add the brisket and cook until heated through, about 5 minutes. Season to taste with salt and serve hot.

WINE NOTES

New World Syrah pairs well with this dish. Try bottlings from Truchard or Cuvaison from California, or a Shiraz from Australia produced by Rosemount or Yangarra.

filetes de res con shiitakes en salsa de morita y tomatillo
beef tenderloin filets with shiitakes in morita chile and tomatillo sauce

The filet mignon is a luxurious cut and deserves to be served in a manner that befits its high standard. In this dish, the small steaks are grilled and served with silken shiitakes in a robust sauce that has been infused with the smoky flavor of morita chiles. A cloak of melted Chihuahua cheese is the finishing touch. **MAKES 6 SERVINGS**

MORITA CHILE AND TOMATILLO SAUCE

2 pounds tomatillos, husked and rinsed

1 cup water

3 to 4 morita or dried chipotle chiles, seeded

¼ cup extra-virgin olive oil

2 pounds shiitakes, stemmed and thinly sliced

Fine sea salt

Six 8-ounce center-cut beef tenderloin filets

Fine sea salt and freshly ground black pepper

6 slices Chihuahua or Monterey Jack cheese

3 tablespoons chopped fresh cilantro for garnish

1. To make the sauce: Position a broiler rack about 6 inches from the source of heat and preheat the broiler. Place the tomatillos on the rack. Broil, turning the tomatillos occasionally, until they are lightly browned on all sides, about 7 minutes. Do not overcook, or the tomatillos will burst. Transfer to a plate and let cool.

2. Bring the water to a boil in a small saucepan over high heat. Add the morita or chipotle chiles, reduce the heat to medium-low, and simmer for 5 minutes, or until the chiles soften. Remove from the heat.

3. Heat the oil in a large skillet over medium-high heat. Add the shiitakes and cook, stirring occasionally, until tender, about 10 minutes. Set aside.

4. Drain the chiles, reserving the soaking liquid. Purée the tomatillos and chiles in a blender, using some of the reserved soaking liquid as needed to smooth the mixture. Transfer to a large saucepan and bring to a boil over medium heat. Add the shiitakes and return to a boil. Reduce the heat to medium-low and simmer to blend the flavors, about 8 minutes. Season to taste with salt. (The mushroom mixture can be prepared 2 hours ahead and kept at room temperature. Reheat before serving.)

5. Prepare a hot fire in a charcoal grill, or preheat a gas grill to high. Meanwhile, remove the beef from the refrigerator, season to taste with salt and pepper, and let stand at room temperature while the grill is heating.

6. Lightly oil the grill grids. Place the beef on the grill, cover, and cook until well browned on the bottom, about 3 minutes. Turn, cover, and cook until the meat feels somewhat firmer than raw when pressed in the center, about 3 minutes longer for medium-rare meat. (If you want to use an instant-read thermometer, insert one horizontally into the side of a filet, as it may be difficult to stand it vertically in the meat. The temperature should register 130°F for medium-rare.) Transfer to a wire rack on a baking sheet and let rest for 5 minutes. (This allows the meat to cook a bit more from residual heat and makes for a juicier steak.)

7. Meanwhile, position the rack about 6 inches from the heat source and preheat the broiler. Top each filet with a slice of cheese. Place them on the broiler rack and broil just until the cheese melts.

8. To serve, place each filet on a warmed dinner plate and surround with mushrooms in sauce, drizzling some of the sauce over the steak. Garnish with the cilantro and serve immediately.

WINE NOTES
Because of the smokiness of the morita chile and the meatiness of the beef, I like to pair this dish with a Syrah from the northern Rhône. Côte-Rôtie, Cornas, and Crozes-Hermitage from producers such as Guigal, Chapoutier, Jean-Luc Colombo, and Jaboulet offer a large range of possibilities.

chuleta de ternera en salsa de frijoles negros y habanero
veal chops with black bean and habanero sauce

There is no Mexican equivalent to the Chinese concept of yin and yang, but if there was, this dish would be an example. Here, delicate grilled veal is brined, then marinated, grilled, and served with a forthright sauce of black beans and chiles, making nuances of layered flavor. **MAKES 4 SERVINGS**

4 double-cut veal rib chops (about 14 ounces each)

Basic Brine for Meats (page 170)

1 cup Guajillo Chile Purée (page 165)

½ cup fresh orange juice

BLACK BEAN AND HABANERO SAUCE

1 cup dried black beans, rinsed and picked over

½ teaspoon fine sea salt

1 habanero chile, seeded, deveined, and minced

3 tablespoons plus ¼ cup canola oil

1 small ripe plantain, peeled and cut into ½-inch-thick diagonal slices

1 ripe avocado, peeled, pitted, and diced

1. A few hours before serving, refrigerate the veal chops in the brine in a large nonreactive bowl for 3 hours, no longer. Drain and pat dry with paper towels.

2. Whisk the Guajillo Chile Purée and orange juice in another large nonreactive bowl. Add the veal and turn to coat. Cover and refrigerate for at least 2 hours or up to 6 hours.

3. To make the sauce: Bring 3 quarts of water to a boil in a large saucepan. Add the beans, reduce the heat to low, and simmer for 1 hour. Add ½ teaspoon salt and simmer until the beans are tender, about 30 minutes more. Scoop out and reserve 1 cup of the cooking liquid. Drain the beans. Transfer half of the cooked beans to a blender. With the machine running, add enough of the reserved cooking liquid to make a smooth purée that is slightly thicker than heavy cream. Transfer to a bowl and stir in the remaining beans. Gradually stir in the habanero chile to taste—it should not overpower the black beans. Season to taste with salt. Transfer to a small saucepan and set aside. (The sauce can be made up to 2 hours ahead and stored at room temperature.)

4. Prepare a hot fire in a charcoal grill and bank the coals, with one area hotter and thicker than the other. For a gas grill, preheat one side to high and the other side to low.

5. While the grill is heating, drain the veal chops but leave some sauce clinging to the meat. Coat with the 3 tablespoons oil and season with salt. Lightly oil the grill grids. Place the veal chops over the hotter area of the grill and cook for 2 minutes. Turn 90 degrees and cook 1 minute longer. Turn the chops over and grill for 2 minutes. Transfer to the cooler side of the grill. Cover the grill and cook until the chops show no sign of pink when pierced at the bone, about 15 minutes.

6. Meanwhile, heat the ¼ cup oil in a large skillet over medium-high heat. Add the plantain and cook until golden on the bottom, about 3 minutes. Turn and cook until golden on the other side, about 2 minutes more. Using a slotted metal spatula, transfer to paper towels to drain briefly.

7. To serve, heat the black bean sauce over medium-low heat until simmering. Spoon equal amounts of the sauce in the center of each of 4 dinner plates. Top each with a veal chop. Garnish with the fried plantain and diced avocado and serve immediately.

WINE NOTES

The beans in this dish need an earthy wine. A French red Burgundy would be overpowered by the habaneros, but Pinot Noirs from Oregon and California are good matches. Try King Estate, Sokol Blosser, or Ponzi, from Oregon; Au Bon Climat, Rochioli, or Saintsbury, from California; or wines made by Martinborough, Palliser, or Isabel Estate, from New Zealand.

chuleta de puerco en salsa de chile ancho
pork chops with ancho-chile sauce

Manchamanteles is one of the famous seven moles of Oaxaca—its name, "tablecloth stainer," refers to the deep red color of the sauce, which will really challenge your laundry detergent if you get it on fabric. This is my version of a dish using this mole, which is made distinctive by the addition of sweet pineapple, plantain, and yam. Because the flavors here are so complex and varied, serve this with White Rice (page 150) or another relatively plain starchy side dish. MAKES 4 SERVINGS

4 double-cut bone-in pork loin chops (about 14 ounces each)

Basic Brine for Meats (page 170)

ANCHO-CHILE SAUCE

1 small yam (orange-fleshed sweet potato)

¼ cup plus 3 tablespoons canola oil

½ small ripe plantain, peeled and cut into ½-inch-thick rounds

Ancho Chile Purée (page 165)

½ teaspoon ground cinnamon

⅛ teaspoon ground cloves

Freshly ground black pepper

Two 1-inch-thick slices fresh pineapple, peeled and cored

1. Refrigerate the pork chops in the brine for 6 hours.

2. Meanwhile, start the sauce: Position a rack in the center of the oven and preheat the oven to 375°F. Pierce the yam in a few places with a fork. Place on a baking sheet and bake until tender, about 45 minutes. Let cool to the touch. Peel, then cut the flesh into bite-size pieces. Set aside.

3. Heat the ¼ cup oil in a large skillet over medium-high heat. Add the plantain and cook until golden on the bottom, about 3 minutes. Turn and cook until golden on the other side, about 2 minutes. Using a slotted metal spatula, transfer to paper towels and set aside. (The yam and plantain can be prepared up to 4 hours ahead, stored at room temperature.)

4. Prepare a hot fire in a charcoal grill and bank the coals, with one area hotter and thicker than the other. For a gas grill, preheat one side to high and the other side to low.

5. Bring the Ancho Chile Purée to a simmer in a large saucepan over medium heat. Add the cinnamon and cloves, reduce the heat to medium-low, and simmer for 5 minutes. Set aside and keep warm.

6. Drain the pork chops and pat dry with paper towels. Coat the pork chops with the 3 tablespoons oil and season to taste with pepper. Lightly oil the grill grids. Place the pork chops over the hotter area of the grill and cover the grill. Cook for 2 minutes, then turn 90 degrees and grill for 1 minute longer. Turn the chops over and grill 2 minutes longer. Transfer them to the cooler side of the grill. Cover and cook until the chops show no sign of pink when pierced at the bone, about 15 minutes. During the last few minutes, place the pineapple slices on the hotter area of the grill and cook, turning once, until seared with grill marks. Transfer the pork chops and pineapple to a platter.

7. Cut the pineapple into bite-size pieces. Add to the sauce along with the yam and plantain and reheat over medium heat until the yam is heated through, about 3 minutes.

8. To serve, spoon some chile sauce in the center of each of 4 dinner plates and top each with a pork chop. Using a slotted spoon, surround the chop with the yam, plantain, and pineapple. Serve hot.

WINE NOTES
This is a very rustic, earthy mole. Tempranillo from Rioja and the Ribero del Duero in Spain will enhance it. Marqués de Murrieta, Montecillo, and La Rioja Alta are excellent examples of the former. From the Ribero, look for wines made by Bodegas Reyes, Alejandro Fernández, or Bodegas Arzuaga Navarro.

mixiote de borrego en mole coloradito
lamb shanks in oaxacan red mole sauce

There are many different varieties of mole, the thick, sweet-savory sauce that is a particular specialty of Oaxaca. Here, meaty lamb shanks and the sauce are wrapped in banana leaves (available at Latino and Asian markets), then roasted until the lamb is falling off the bone. Served with Pinto Beans with Bacon and Poblano Chiles (page 149), this is a perfect dish for a cold blustery night, which aren't too common in Oaxaca, but we have plenty of them in Chicago. MAKES 4 SERVINGS

RED MOLE SAUCE

8 ancho chiles, seeded and deveined

6 guajillo chiles, seeded and deveined

1 tablespoon sesame seeds

¼ teaspoon black peppercorns

½ teaspoon dried oregano

2 unpeeled garlic cloves

6 plum (Roma) tomatoes, roasted (see page 26)

3 tablespoons canola oil

½ cup sugar

1½ ounces Mexican chocolate, coarsely chopped

½ teaspoon ground cinnamon

Salt

½ cup canola oil

Four 1- to 1¼-pound lamb shanks

Salt and freshly ground black pepper

Four 12-inch squares thawed frozen banana leaves

4 tablespoons red wine vinegar

½ onion, chopped

1. To make the mole: Put the ancho and guajillo chiles in a medium bowl and add boiling water to cover. Let stand until the chiles soften, about 20 minutes.

2. Meanwhile, heat a small, heavy skillet, preferably cast iron, over medium heat. Add the sesame seeds and cook, stirring often, until toasted, about 3 minutes. Transfer to a plate. Add the peppercorns to the skillet and cook until they smell toasted, about 1 minute; add to the sesame seeds. Add the oregano to the skillet and cook, stirring until fragrant, about 1 minute; add to the sesame and peppercorns. Let cool, then grind the mixture coarsely in a spice grinder or mortar. Add the garlic to the skillet and increase the heat to medium-high. Cook the garlic, turning occasionally, until the skins are browned, about 3 minutes. Let cool, then peel.

3. Purée the tomatoes and garlic in a blender, adding a little water if needed to create a moderately thick, saucelike consistency. Set aside.

4. When the chiles are soft, drain them, reserving the soaking water. Purée the chiles in a blender, adding a little reserved soaking water as needed to make a thick sauce. Strain the purée through a sieve.

5. Heat the oil in a medium saucepan over medium heat. Add the sesame seed mixture and stir until fragrant but not browned, about 15 seconds. Stir in the chile and tomato purées (be careful, they

will splatter) and bring to a boil. Stir in the sugar, chocolate, and cinnamon and reduce the heat to medium-low. Simmer briskly, stirring often, until the sauce is lightly thickened, adding more water if it gets too thick, about 20 minutes. Season to taste with salt. Set aside and let cool slightly.

6. To prepare the lamb shanks: Position a rack in the center of the oven and preheat the oven to 350°F. Heat the oil in a large skillet over high heat. Season the lamb to taste with the salt and pepper. In batches, without crowding, add the lamb to the skillet and brown on all sides, and then transfer to a platter.

7. One at a time, dip a lamb shank in the mole to coat on all sides. Place on a banana leaf and sprinkle with 1 tablespoon of the vinegar and one-fourth of the onion. Season the onion lightly with salt. Wrap like a package in the banana leaf. Over-wrap with aluminum foil. Cover and refrigerate the remaining mole until ready to serve.

8. Place the packets in a roasting pan and bake until the meat is falling off the bone, about 3½ hours.

9. To serve, reheat the reserved mole sauce and transfer to a sauceboat. Unwrap the lamb, discarding the foil. Place the lamb in its banana leaf on each dinner plate and serve hot, with the sauce passed on the side.

WINE NOTES

The sweet flavors in the sauce (cinnamon and chocolate) and the combination of both ancho and guajillo chiles is enhanced when paired with Châteauneuf-du-Pape. Producers to look for are Chapoutier, Château de Beaucastel, Vieux Télégraphe, and Guigal. An Australian Grenache (Clarendon Hills, Henschke, Yangarra, or d'Arenberg) is an option.

costillitas de borrego con corteza de pepitas
baby racks of lamb with a pumpkin-seed crust

This dish is a perfect illustration of how the right wine can match Mexican food. In fact, it's hard for me to even think of rack of lamb without a red wine to go with it. The pumpkin-seed crust is much more flavorful than the typical bread crumb coating for lamb, and the crunchy texture is more interesting, too. MAKES 4 SERVINGS

PASILLA-TOMATILLO SAUCE

8 pasilla chiles, seeded, deveined, and toasted (see page 23)

4 large garlic cloves, crushed

1½ cups water

1 cup Roasted Tomatillo Sauce (page 165)

Fine sea salt

¼ cup canola oil

Four 8-ounce baby racks of lamb, bones frenched

Fine sea salt and freshly ground black pepper

½ cup honey, heated until liquid

1 cup shelled pumpkin seeds (pepitas), toasted (see page 26) and pulsed in a food processor until coarsely chopped

1. To make the sauce: Purée the chiles, garlic, and water in a blender. Strain through a sieve into a medium saucepan. Stir in the Roasted Tomatillo Sauce and bring to a boil over medium heat. Season to taste with salt. Set aside. (The sauce can be made up to 1 day ahead, cooled, covered, and refrigerated. Reheat before serving.)

2. Position a rack in the top third of the oven and preheat the oven to 450°F.

3. Heat the oil in a large, heavy skillet over medium-high heat. Season the lamb racks to taste with salt and pepper. Add the racks to the skillet, meaty side down, and cook until browned, about 5 minutes. Stand the racks on end and brown one end and then the other, about 1 minute per end. Place on a rack in a roasting pan and transfer to the oven. Roast for about 15 minutes, or until an instant-read thermometer inserted in the thickest part of a rack reads 130°F for medium-rare.

4. Remove from the oven, tent loosely with aluminum foil, and let rest for 8 to 10 minutes so the juices can settle. Heat the honey in a small saucepan or in a microwave oven just until liquid. Brush the honey over the lamb and coat with the crushed pumpkin seeds.

5. To serve, spoon some of the Pasilla-Tomatillo Sauce in the center of each of 4 dinner plates. Cut each rack in half crosswise and arrange the halves on the plates. Serve hot.

WINE NOTES
A Cabernet Sauvignon with moderate tannins complements this dish superbly. Try one from California such as Souverain or Chateau St. Jean. Columbia Crest from Washington is equally delicious.

chuletas de borrego en salsa de pasilla
lamb loin chops in garlicky pasilla sauce

The loin of the lamb is the most elegant cut, compact and tender but flavorful. Loin chops are perfect for dinner parties (and busy restaurants), as they don't take much time to cook. They are best served with a simple sauce that doesn't overshadow the meat. This pasilla sauce is a fine match with grilled chops, especially with Spinach Tamales (page 154) on the side. **MAKES 4 SERVINGS**

PASILLA SAUCE

8 pasilla chiles, seeded, deveined, and toasted (see page 23)

4 large garlic cloves, crushed

1½ cups water

Salt

Eight 6-ounce lamb loin chops, cut about 1½ inches thick

¼ cup olive oil

Salt and freshly ground black pepper

1. Prepare a hot fire in a charcoal grill, or preheat a gas grill to high.

2. To make the sauce: Purée the chiles, garlic, and water in a blender until smooth. Season to taste with salt. Transfer to a small saucepan and bring to a boil, stirring often, over medium heat. Keep the sauce warm.

3. Coat the lamb chops with the oil and season to taste with salt and pepper. Lightly oil the grill grids. Grill the chops for 2 minutes. Rotate the chops 90 degrees and cook for another 2 minutes. Turn the chops over and grill for 2 minutes. Turn the chops on their sides to brown, 1 or 2 minutes more. Transfer the chops to a platter and let stand for 5 minutes.

4. Spoon a few tablespoons of the Pasilla Sauce onto each of 4 dinner plates. Top each with 2 chops and serve immediately.

WINE NOTES
The garlicky, earthy Pasilla Sauce is a great match for Nebbiolo. Barolos tend to be too tannic, but Barbarescos work well, especially those produced by Vietti, Bruno Giacosa, or Ceretto.

mole de jengibre con pechugas de pollo
chicken breasts in ginger mole

The mild but distinct spiciness of ginger marries well with the heat of chiles, as this new-style mole shows. There is enough sauce for eight chicken breasts, so you could double the number of breasts to serve a large group, or use the leftover sauce for another meal. (It makes a great barbecue sauce to slather on pork chops during the last few minutes of grilling.) If, however, you serve the breasts with a side dish that likes a good dousing of sauce, like white rice, or if you offer a stack of warm corn tortillas for dipping, you may not have any sauce left over after all. **MAKES 4 SERVINGS**

GINGER MOLE

2 ancho chiles, seeded and deveined

1 pasilla chile, seeded and deveined

2 guajillo chiles, seeded and deveined

1 plum (Roma) tomato

½ white onion

2 garlic cloves

2 tablespoons peeled and shredded fresh ginger (use the large holes of a box grater)

¼ cup sesame seeds, toasted (see page 26)

1 teaspoon black peppercorns

2 cups water

2 tablespoons canola oil

Fine sea salt

Four 7-ounce skinless, boneless chicken breast halves, lightly pounded to an even thickness

Fine sea salt and freshly ground black pepper

2 tablespoons canola oil

Sesame seeds for garnish

1. To make the mole: Heat a large, dry skillet over medium-high heat. Add the ancho chiles to the skillet and cook, turning them occasionally, until they soften, give off their aroma, and show some darker spots, about 2 minutes. Do not overtoast the chiles or they will taste bitter. Repeat with the pasilla and guajillo chiles.

2. Position a broiler rack about 6 inches from the source of heat and preheat the broiler. Place the tomato, onion half, and garlic on the rack. Broil, turning occasionally, transferring to a plate as they are ready: **Onion Half:** Broil until the edges are browned and the onion softens, about 5 minutes. **Tomato:** Broil just until the skin is charred and peeling, about 5 minutes. **Garlic:** Broil until the skins are browned, about 7 minutes.

3. Purée the anchos, pasilla, and guajillo chiles, ginger, tomato, onion, garlic, sesame seeds, peppercorns, and water in a blender, in batches if necessary. Heat the oil in a medium saucepan over medium-high heat. Add the mole (be careful, as it will splatter) and bring to a boil. Reduce the heat to medium-low and simmer, stirring often, until slightly thickened, about 10 minutes. Season to taste with salt. Set aside and keep warm. (The mole can be made up to 4 hours ahead and stored at room temperature. Or, let cool, cover, and refrigerate for up to 3 days. Reheat before serving.)

4. One at a time, place a chicken breast between two plastic bags. Using a flat meat mallet or a rolling pin, lightly pound the chicken breast so it is evenly thick. Season to taste with salt and pepper.

5. Heat the oil in a large skillet over medium-high heat. Add the chicken breasts to the skillet and cook until golden brown on the bottom, about 4 minutes. Turn, reduce the heat to medium, and cook until the chicken is golden brown on the second side and feels firm when pressed in the center, about 4 minutes.

6. To serve, place a chicken breast on each of 4 dinner plates. Spoon some mole on top and sprinkle with the sesame seeds. Serve hot.

WINE NOTES
The spicy notes in the mole go well with a Pinot Gris from Alsace. Particularly good would be one produced by Zind-Humbrecht, Weinbach, or Hugel. Pinot Gris from Oregon also works well. Look for those made by WillaKenzie, Bethel Heights, or Ponzi.

pollitos con salsa de guajillo
baby chickens with guajillo sauce

In Morelia a deep-fried chicken dish is served by street vendors and in market stalls. A sort of an open-faced enchilada, it is delicious, but very heavy. I wanted the same flavors, but lighter, and this is my interpretation. Whenever this is on the menu at ¡Salpicón!, I find it hard to eat anything else. MAKES 4 SERVINGS

4 baby chickens (poussins)

3 cups Guajillo Chile Purée (page 165)

1 red-skinned potato, peeled and cut into ½-inch dice

1 carrot, peeled and cut into ½-inch dice

Fine sea salt

¼ cup canola oil

8 corn tortillas

1 cup crumbled fresh goat cheese for garnish

⅓ cup finely chopped white onion for garnish

1. Using kitchen shears, cut down one side of the backbone of each chicken. Open up the chicken and flatten it to butterfly. Combine the chickens and 1 cup of the Guajillo Chile Purée in a large bowl. Turn to coat. Cover and refrigerate for at least 4 hours or up to 8 hours.

2. Bring a medium saucepan of lightly salted water to a boil over high heat. Add the potato and cook over medium heat until barely tender, about 20 minutes. Using a slotted spoon, remove the potato and set aside. Add the carrot to the water and cook until barely tender, about 6 minutes. Drain and set aside. (The potato and carrot can be prepared up to 4 hours ahead and stored at room temperature.)

3. Prepare a hot fire in a charcoal grill and push the coals to one side of the grill. On a gas grill, have one area on high and the other side off.

4. Remove the chickens from the marinade and season to taste with salt. Lightly oil the grill grids. Place the chickens on the cool area of the grill, skin side down, and cover. Grill until the chickens show no sign of pink when pierced at the thigh, about 20 minutes. Transfer to a platter and tent with aluminum foil to keep warm.

5. Meanwhile, preheat the oven to 200°F. When ready to serve, heat the canola oil in a medium skillet over medium-high heat. Pour the remaining

2 cups Guajillo Chile Purée into a shallow dish (a pie pan works well) and place it, and a nonstick baking sheet, near the stove. Working quickly, dip a tortilla into the sauce, then shake off the excess sauce. Transfer to the hot oil and cook for a few seconds, turn, then cook until the tortilla is soft enough to fold, a few seconds longer. Put the tortilla on the baking sheet and fold it into quarters. Repeat with the remaining tortillas and sauce. Keep the sauced, folded tortillas warm in the oven.

6. Pour the remaining sauce into a medium saucepan and bring to a boil over medium heat. Add the potato and carrot and cook until heated through, about 3 minutes.

7. To serve, place 2 folded tortillas in the center of each of 4 dinner plates. Cut each chicken in half lengthwise and place the two halves over each other on top of the tortillas. Using a slotted spoon, surround the chickens with the vegetables, then a drizzle of sauce. Sprinkle with the cheese and onions, and serve hot.

WINE NOTES
The guajillo sauce with the chicken is well matched with a Sangiovese from Tuscany. Try a Chianti Classico produced by Antinori, Badia a Coltibuono, or Querciabella.

pato almendrado
duck two ways in ancho-almond sauce

There's nothing really wrong with a whole roast duck, even though the breast gets a bit overdone. Like many cooks, however, I prefer to prepare the breast and legs separately with methods that show them at their best. This way, you can sauté the duck breast until it is medium-rare with a crisp skin, and make a duck confit with the legs. (You will need 2 large skillets to sauté the duck breasts without crowding them.) An almond mole pulls the parts together. Potatoes with Spinach and Onions (page 145) is a great side for this dish. You will find duck legs and duck fat at specialty markets, or you can order them from D'Artagnan (see Sources, page 187) **MAKES 6 SERVINGS**

DUCK CONFIT

1 cup kosher salt

⅓ cup plus 1 tablespoon coarsely chopped garlic

25 thyme sprigs

1 tablespoon coarsely ground black pepper

6 duck leg quarters

6 cups rendered duck fat (See Sources, page 187)

ALMOND MOLE

2 ancho chiles, seeded and deveined

3 cups boiling water

2 ripe tomatoes, roasted (see page 26)

½ cup natural almonds

¼ cup unsalted peanuts

2 garlic cloves

½-inch piece cinnamon stick

3 cloves

Fine sea salt

3 duck breast halves, skin scored in a crosshatch pattern

Fine sea salt and freshly ground black pepper

2 tablespoons canola oil

½ cup nonpareil capers, drained and rinsed

1. To make the confit: At least 1 day before serving, mix the salt, garlic, thyme, and pepper in a small bowl. Place the duck legs in a roasting pan just large enough to hold them in 1 layer. Sprinkle both sides with the salt mixture. Cover with plastic wrap and refrigerate overnight.

2. Position a rack in the center of the oven and preheat the oven to 300°F.

3. Brush off most of the salt mixture from the duck legs, leaving some of it as a seasoning. Melt the duck fat in a medium saucepan over low heat. Pour the duck fat over the duck legs and cover with aluminum foil. Bake until the meat is falling off the bone, about 1¾ hours. Remove the duck from the fat to a plate and set aside. (Or, to make up to 5 days ahead, let the duck legs cool in the fat

in the roasting pan, then cover and refrigerate. Remove the duck from the cold fat and scrape off the clinging fat. Bake in a preheated 350°F oven on a baking sheet until heated through, about 30 minutes.)

4. To make the mole: Soak the chiles in the boiling water in a small bowl until they soften. Drain, reserving the soaking liquid.

5. Purée the chiles, tomatoes, almonds, peanuts, garlic, cinnamon, and cloves in a blender, adding 2½ cups of the reserved chile soaking liquid. Strain through a sieve into a heavy, medium saucepan. Bring to a boil over medium heat, stirring often. Reduce the heat to medium-low and simmer, stirring almost constantly, until the sauce thickens and is reduced to about 2 cups, about 20 minutes. Season to taste with salt. (The sauce can be made 1 day ahead, cooled, covered, and refrigerated. Reheat over low heat, adding water if needed to return the sauce to its original consistency.)

recipe continues

6. Season the duck breasts to taste with salt and pepper. Add 1 tablespoon oil to each of 2 large nonstick skillets and heat over medium-high heat. Add the duck breasts, skin side down, and cook until deep golden-brown on the bottom, about 4 minutes. Turn and reduce the heat to medium. Cook for about 4 minutes, or until the meat feels only slightly resistant when pressed in the center for medium-rare. Transfer to a carving board, tent with aluminum foil, and let rest for 5 minutes.

7. Pour the duck fat out of the skillets into a heatproof bowl. Return the skillets to medium-high heat. Add the duck legs, skin side down, to the skillet and cook until the skin crisps, about 5 minutes.

8. To serve, cut each breast across the grain into ½-inch-thick diagonal slices. Spoon about ¼ cup sauce onto each of 6 dinner plates. Top each with equal amounts of breast slices, fanning out the slices, then a duck leg. Garnish with the capers. Serve immediately.

WINE NOTES

This is one dish that works equally well with white or red wine. For white, choose an Alsatian Gewürztraminer or a Pinot Gris, preferably from Zind-Humbrecht, Domaine Weinbach, Marcel Deiss, or Hugel. For reds, Merlot-based wines make a great pairing. From Bordeaux, Château Canon and Château La Gaffelière, both from St. Emilion, are excellent. Look for Lewis Cellars and Pride Mountain Vineyards from California.

pierna de pato con granada
duck leg confit with pomegranate

Pomegranates are much appreciated in Mexico for their bright red color and sweet-tart juice. They used to be a fairly unusual fruit in America, but no more. You can get pomegranate juice everywhere, and while the fresh fruit once appeared in the market for only a few weeks in autumn, it now shows up almost all year round. Here it is combined with orange and chiles to make a beautiful sauce to dress shredded duck leg confit. This makes a nice luncheon entreé or dinner appetizer. You will find duck legs and duck fat at specialty markets, or you can order them from D'Artagnan (see Sources, page 187) **MAKES 6 SERVINGS**

DUCK CONFIT

½ cup kosher salt

3 tablespoons coarsely chopped garlic

15 thyme sprigs

1½ teaspoons coarsely ground black pepper

3 duck leg quarters

3 cups duck fat

POMEGRANATE-ORANGE SAUCE

1 cup Four-Chile Sauce (page 166)

½ cup bottled pomegranate juice (plain, without other fruit flavors)

½ cup fresh orange juice

Fine sea salt

¾ cup pomegranate seeds (arils, see Note)

1 navel orange, peeled and segmented (see page 90) for garnish

Warm corn tortillas for serving

1. To make the confit: At least 1 day before serving, mix the salt, garlic, thyme, and pepper in a small bowl. Place the duck legs in a roasting pan just large enough to hold them. Sprinkle both sides with the salt mixture. Cover with plastic wrap and refrigerate overnight.

2. Position a rack in the center of the oven and preheat the oven to 300°F.

3. Brush off most of the salt mixture from the duck legs, leaving some of it as a seasoning. Melt the duck fat in a medium saucepan over low heat. Pour the duck fat over the duck legs and cover with aluminum foil. Bake until the meat is falling off the bone, about 1¾ hours. (Or, to make up to 5 days ahead, let the duck legs cool in the fat in the roasting pan, then cover and refrigerate. Remove the duck from the fat and scrape off the clinging fat. Bake in a preheated 350°F oven on a baking

sheet until heated through, about 30 minutes.) Transfer the duck to a plate and let cool to the touch. Remove and reserve the skin. Using 2 forks, shred the duck meat and set aside.

4. Heat a large nonstick skillet over medium-high heat. Add the duck skin and cook, stirring occasionally, until brown and crisp, about 8 minutes. Transfer the duck skin to paper towels to cool. Crumble the duck skin. (The duck skin and shredded duck can be prepared up to 2 hours ahead and stored at room temperature. Reheat the shredded duck in a nonstick skillet over medium heat, stirring occasionally, until heated through, about 5 minutes. Use the duck skin at room temperature.)

5. To make the sauce: Bring the Four-Chile Sauce to a boil in a heavy, medium saucepan over medium heat, stirring often. Stir in the pomegranate and orange juices and return to a boil. Reduce the heat to medium-low and simmer, stirring almost constantly, until the sauce is reduced to 1 cup. Season to taste with salt. (The sauce can be prepared up to 2 hours ahead and stored at room temperature. Reheat before using.)

recipe continues

6. To serve, stir enough of the duck sauce into the duck meat to moisten it; reserve the remaining sauce. Stir the pomegranate seeds into the duck mixture. For each serving, place a 3-inch-round metal ring mold (or biscuit cutter) in the center of a dinner plate. Scoop the duck mixture into the ring mold, pack down lightly, and sprinkle with some of the crisp skin. Lift up the ring. Spoon a bit of the reserved sauce around the confit and garnish with orange segments. Serve immediately, with warm corn tortillas.

NOTE: Removing pomegranate seeds (the juice-filled capsules that surround the seeds are actually called arils) from the fruit itself can be a little messy, and pomegranate juice will stain. Here's a squirt-free way to do this job. Cut a shallow *X*, about ¼ inch deep, into the blossom end of the fruit. Fill a large bowl full of water and immerse the fruit in the water. Holding the fruit under the water, use the scored *X* to pull the fruit apart into quarters. Gently work the seeds away from the thin membrane. Discard any membrane floating on the water—it is very bitter. Drain the seeds in a sieve.

WINE NOTES

The sweet-tart notes of this sauce pairs nicely with a juicy California Zinfandel, in particular those made by Ridge, Brown Estate, and Truchard. Australian Shiraz also works well, such as one produced by Rosemount, d'Arenberg, Penfolds, or Henschke.

codornices en salsa de chile ancho y miel
grilled quail with ancho-honey sauce

The ancho is one of the most versatile chiles in the Capsicum family, as it has a relatively mild heat level, with a hint of sweetness as a background note. Here it is used both in the marinade for the quail and in the sauce. You can grind the chiles yourself, or substitute ½ cup pure ground ancho chile (see Sources, page 187). Quail are very lean and will dry out if overcooked, so grill them only to the medium-rare stage, as they will continue to cook a bit more off the grill. Scalloped Potatoes (page 146) make a rich accompaniment to the grilled quail. MAKES 4 SERVINGS

CHILE OIL

6 or 7 ancho chiles, seeded, deveined, and toasted (see page 23)

1 cup olive oil

1 head garlic, cloves peeled and chopped (¼ cup)

8 semi-boneless quail

Fine sea salt

1 cup Ancho-Honey Sauce (page 166)

Scalloped Potatoes (page 146)

1. To make the Chile Oil: At least 6 hours before serving, use an electric spice grinder to grind the chiles in batches into a powder. Whisk the chile powder, oil, and garlic together in a medium glass or stainless-steel bowl.

2. Add the quail to the Chile Oil and turn to coat. Cover and refrigerate for at least 6 hours or up to 12 hours. Remove the quail from the refrigerator 1 hour before grilling.

3. Prepare a hot fire in a charcoal grill, or preheat a gas grill to high.

4. Remove the quail from the Chile Oil, draining them well (excess oil will drip onto the coals or heat source and cause flare-ups) but leaving the marinade clinging to the quail. Season the quail to taste with salt. Lightly oil the grill grids. Place the quail, skin side down, on the grill. Cover the grill and cook until browned on the bottom, about 4 minutes. Turn and grill until the quail are browned on the second side and the thigh joint remains somewhat pink when pierced with the tip of a sharp knife, about 2 minutes. Transfer to a platter, tent with aluminum foil, and let stand for 5 minutes (the quail will continue to cook a bit more from their residual heat).

5. For each serving, spread about ¼ cup of the Ancho-Honey Sauce on a dinner plate and top with 2 quail. Serve immediately with Scalloped Potatoes.

WINE NOTES

The sauce on this dish requires a big, fruit-forward wine with low tannin levels, and the following California Zinfandels fit the bill: Cosentino, Burgess, Ridge, and Brown Estate. From Australia, try a Shiraz by either Rosemount, Yangarra, d'Arenberg, or Penfolds.

guarniciones
side dishes

rajas con crema
roasted poblano strips with cream

The title of this side dish is slightly misleading, because along with the mildly spicy poblano strips, you'll also find corn and tomatoes. The result is a kind of creamy stew that goes well with simply prepared entrées—it can even serve as a sauce for grilled chicken breast. Serve it with warm tortillas, because you won't want to leave a drop behind on your plate. MAKES 4 TO 6 SERVINGS

4 poblano chiles, roasted and peeled (see page 22)

2 tablespoons olive oil

1 large white onion, cut into thin half-moons

6 garlic cloves, finely chopped

4 ripe plum (Roma) tomatoes, peeled, seeded (see page 26), and diced

1 tablespoon finely chopped fresh thyme

2 or 3 ears of corn, kernels cut off (1 cup)

1 cup Mexican crema or crème fraîche

Fine sea salt

1. Cut the chiles into ¼-inch-thick strips and set aside.

2. Heat the oil in a medium skillet over medium-high heat. Add the onion and cook, stirring often, until translucent, about 4 minutes. Stir in the garlic and cook until fragrant, about 1 minute. Stir in the poblano strips, tomatoes, and thyme. Reduce the heat to medium-low, cover, and cook until the tomatoes give off their juices, about 5 minutes. Stir in the corn and cook until heated through, about 2 minutes. Stir in the crema and cook until hot but not boiling, a minute or two longer. Season to taste with salt. Serve hot.

papas con chorizo
potatoes with chorizo

These addictive potatoes are the perfect side dish for the Baby Racks of Lamb with a Pumpkin-Seed Crust on page 127, but that is just the beginning. They are fantastic for breakfast or brunch, served alongside scrambled eggs. Be sure to use soft Mexican chorizo here, not the hard, smoked Spanish-style links.
MAKES 4 SERVINGS

2 unpeeled baking potatoes (about 1 pound), scrubbed

8 ounces Mexican chorizo, removed from casings

Fine sea salt

1. Put the potatoes in a large saucepan and cover with lightly salted water. Bring to a boil over high heat. Reduce the heat to medium-low and simmer until the potatoes are barely tender, 20 to 30 minutes. Drain and rinse under cold water until cool to the touch. Peel the potatoes and cut into ½-inch dice. (The potatoes can be prepared up to 1 day ahead, cooled, covered, and refrigerated.)

2. Cook the chorizo in a medium nonstick skillet over medium heat, breaking up the meat with the side of a spoon, until it is dark red and most of the fat has been released, about 15 minutes. Stir in the potatoes and cook, stirring occasionally, until the potatoes are heated through, 3 to 5 minutes. Season to taste with salt. Serve hot.

papas con espinaca y cebollas
potatoes with spinach and onions

This recipe provides both a starch and a leafy green in the same bowl. Serve it with grilled or sautéed meats when you'd rather not make 2 side dishes. It is especially good with Duck Two Ways in Ancho-Almond Sauce (page 133). MAKES 4 TO 6 SERVINGS

3 unpeeled baking potatoes (about 1½ pounds), scrubbed

⅓ cup olive oil

½ small white onion, chopped

1 serrano chile, seeded, deveined, and minced

10 ounces fresh spinach, stemmed

Fine sea salt

1. Put the potatoes in a large saucepan and cover with lightly salted water. Bring to a boil over high heat. Reduce the heat to medium-low and simmer until the potatoes are barely tender, 20 to 30 minutes. Drain and rinse under cold water until easy to handle. Peel the potatoes and cut into ½-inch dice. (The potatoes can be prepared up to 1 day ahead, cooled, covered, and refrigerated.)

2. Heat the oil in a large nonstick skillet over medium-high heat. Add the onion and cook, stirring often, until softened, about 3 minutes. Stir in the chile and cook until it begins to soften, about 1 minute. Add the potatoes and cook, stirring occasionally, until heated through, about 2 minutes. Stir in the spinach and cook until wilted, about 1 minute. Remove from the heat and season with salt to taste. Serve hot.

papas con crema y queso añejo
scalloped potatoes

These are my "Mexican" interpretation of scalloped potatoes. They are a rich, but elegant accompaniment to any grilled meats. In the restaurant we serve them with our Grilled Quail with Ancho-Honey Sauce (page 139). But they are so popular that many people just ask if they can order a side of the "quail cakes"! You'll notice that no salt is added to the dish because the cheese is salty enough. MAKES 6 SERVINGS

6 peeled baking potatoes
(about 3 pounds)

1 cup grated queso añejo,
(about 4 ounces)

1 cup chopped cilantro
(about one bunch)

6 ounces heavy cream

1 tablespoon unsalted butter

1. With a kitchen mandolin slice the potatoes lengthwise ¼ inch thick. Rinse the potato slices under cold running water until the water runs clear. Using a kitchen towel, remove the excess water. In a big bowl mix the potatoes, queso añejo, cilantro, and cream.

2. Grease an 8-inch-square baking dish with the butter. Layer the bottom of the dish with about one-third of the potato mixture, and repeat with the rest of the potatoes. Cover with foil.

3. Position a rack in the center of the oven and preheat the oven to 375°F. Bake the potatoes for 1 hour. Remove from the oven and let rest for 20 minutes before serving. With a 3-inch cookie cutter, cut and shape into serving portions. Serve immediately.

tortas de papa con queso añejo
potato cakes with aged mexican cheese

These are basically potato croquettes shaped into triangles. They are a great accompaniment to the Black Sea Bass with Mushrooms and Two Sauces (page 101), but they also are excellent served with different dipping salsas such as the Avocado-Tomatillo Sauce (page 162), the Ancho-Honey Sauce (page 166), or the Roasted Tomato–Chipotle Sauce (page 161). Try them with all three. MAKES 8 POTATO CAKES

2 unpeeled baking potatoes
(about 1 pound), scrubbed

¼ cup all-purpose flour plus
extra for dusting the work table

1 large egg, lightly beaten

¼ cup grated queso añejo
(aged Mexican cheese)

Fine sea salt

¼ cup extra-virgin olive oil

1. Put the potatoes in a large saucepan and cover with lightly salted water. Bring to a boil over high heat. Reduce the heat to medium-low and simmer until the potatoes are barely tender, 20 to 30 minutes. Drain and rinse under cold water until cool to the touch. Peel the potatoes and mash in a medium bowl. While the potatoes are still warm, incorporate the flour, egg, cheese, and salt to taste. On a lightly floured surface, shape the potato mixture into 3-inch triangles, ½ inch thick.

2. In a nonstick sauté pan or skillet, heat the oil to medium heat. Add the potato cakes and cook until light golden brown, about 2 minutes per side. Remove from the pan with a slotted spatula and place on a paper towel to drain. Serve immediately.

frijoles maneados
pinto beans with chihuahua cheese and chiles

The relatively bland flavor of pinto beans gives the cook almost unlimited leeway with flavorings. This recipe is one of my favorites, with melted cheese adding richness, and a garnish of fried serrano chiles. **MAKES 6 TO 8 SERVINGS**

2 cups (1 pound) dried pinto beans, rinsed and picked over

1½ teaspoons fine sea salt plus more to taste

2 cups (8 ounces) shredded Chihuahua or Monterey Jack cheese

2 tablespoons canola oil

6 serrano chiles

1. Put the beans in a large pot and add 3 quarts cold water. Bring to a boil over medium heat. Reduce the heat to medium-low and simmer, uncovered, for 1 hour. Stir in the 1½ teaspoons salt and continue simmering until the beans are tender, about 30 minutes. Drain the beans, reserving the cooking water. Put the cooked beans and about 1 cup of the reserved cooking water in a food processor and pulse about 5 times, leaving the consistency chunky. (The beans can be cooled, covered, and refrigerated for up to 1 day.)

2. Transfer the beans to a medium nonstick saucepan. Cook over medium-low heat until steaming. Stir in the cheese and cook, stirring often, until it is completely melted, about 3 minutes. Remove from the heat. Season with salt to taste. Transfer to a serving bowl.

3. Meanwhile, heat the oil in a small skillet over high heat until it shimmers. Add the chiles and cook, turning occasionally, until blistered but not blackened, about 3 minutes. Using a slotted spoon, garnish the beans with the chiles and serve immediately.

frijoles charros
pinto beans with bacon and poblano chiles

With bits of smoky bacon and mild poblano chiles running throughout them, these beans are almost a meal in themselves. The recipe is from northern Mexico, home to many cattle ranches (*charro* means "cowboy" in Spanish), where the food is relatively free of sauces. Therefore side dishes are extra flavorful to provide interest to the meal. **MAKES 6 TO 8 SERVINGS**

2 cups (1 pound) dried pinto beans, rinsed and picked over

3 quarts water

1½ teaspoons fine sea salt plus more to taste

8 ounces bacon, cut into ¼-inch-long crosswise pieces

3 poblano chiles, seeded, deveined, and chopped

1 white onion, chopped

4 ripe plum (Roma) tomatoes, seeded (see page 26) and diced

1. Put the beans in a large pot and add the water. Bring to a boil over medium heat. Reduce the heat to medium-low and simmer, uncovered, for 1 hour. Stir in the 1½ teaspoons salt and remove from the heat.

2. Cook the bacon in a flameproof casserole or Dutch oven over medium heat until almost crisp, about 8 minutes. Add the chiles and onion and cook, stirring often, until tender, about 10 minutes. Stir in the beans with their cooking liquid and the tomatoes. If needed, add enough cold water to cover the beans and bring to a boil over high heat. Reduce the heat to medium-low and partially cover the pan. Simmer, stirring occasionally, until the beans are tender, about 30 minutes. Season with salt to taste. (The beans can be made up to 2 days ahead, cooled, covered, and refrigerated. Reheat over medium heat, adding more water as needed to return the beans to their somewhat soupy consistency.) Serve hot.

arroz blanco
white rice

This is not a boring plain white rice, as it is loaded with flavor from the onion and garlic. Follow this recipe and you will have great rice worth serving with your finest entrées. Don't skip the soaking step, as it moistens the rice grains to help keep them fluffy and separate. The recipe uses a good amount of oil, but don't be concerned, as it is drained off later. MAKES 4 TO 6 SERVINGS

1½ cups long-grain white rice

1 cup canola oil

1 white onion, cut into 8 wedges

8 garlic cloves, peeled and left whole

2 cups water

1 tablespoon fine sea salt

1. Put the rice in a medium bowl and add 4 cups boiling water. Let soak for 1 hour. Drain in a sieve. Rinse the rice under cold running water until the water runs clear. Drain well for about 5 minutes.

2. Heat the oil in a heavy, medium saucepan over medium heat. Add the rice, onion, and garlic and cook, stirring constantly, until the onion is tender and the rice is evenly opaque, about 12 minutes. Pour the rice mixture into the sieve and drain well.

3. Return the rice mixture to the saucepan. Add the water and salt and bring to a boil over high heat. Reduce the heat to low and cover. Simmer until the rice is tender and the liquid is absorbed, about 20 minutes. Remove from the heat and let stand, covered, for 5 minutes. Serve immediately.

arroz a la poblana
rice with poblano chiles

Here is a variation on the white rice theme, this time with mild poblano chiles delivering flavor. You can substitute a green bell pepper or 2 Italian frying peppers, if you wish. Note that while the rice is sautéed in lots of oil, it is drained off before the final steaming. MAKES 6 SERVINGS

1½ cups long-grain white rice

3 poblano chiles, seeded, deveined, and coarsely chopped

1 white onion, coarsely chopped

4 garlic cloves, coarsely chopped

1 cup canola oil

2 cups water

1 tablespoon fine sea salt

1. Put the rice in a medium bowl and add 4 cups boiling water. Let soak for 1 hour. Drain in a sieve. Rinse the rice under cold running water until the water runs clear. Drain well for about 5 minutes.

2. While the rice is soaking, purée the poblanos, onion, and garlic in a blender and set the purée aside.

3. Heat the oil in a heavy, medium saucepan over medium heat. Add the rice and cook, stirring constantly, until it is evenly opaque, about 12 minutes. Pour the rice into the sieve and drain well to remove the excess oil.

4. Return the rice mixture to the saucepan. Add the poblano purée, water, and salt. Bring to a boil over high heat. Reduce the heat to low and cover. Simmer until the rice is tender and the liquid is absorbed, about 20 minutes. Remove from the heat and let stand, covered, for 5 minutes. Serve immediately.

arroz mexicano
mexican rice

Everyone loves this rice with tomatoes and peas, colored like the Mexican flag in red and green hues. Be sure the tomatoes are good and ripe. If they aren't, you can substitute 1 cup drained canned plum tomatoes.

MAKES 4 TO 6 SERVINGS

1½ cups long-grain white rice

2 large ripe plum (Roma) tomatoes, coarsely chopped

½ white onion, coarsely chopped

2 garlic cloves, coarsely chopped

1 cup canola oil

⅓ cup shelled fresh peas or frozen petite peas

1½ cups water

1 tablespoon fine sea salt

1. Put the rice in a medium bowl and add 4 cups boiling water. Let soak for 1 hour. Drain in a sieve. Rinse the rice under cold running water until the water runs clear. Drain well for about 5 minutes.

2. While the rice is soaking, purée the tomatoes, onion, and garlic in a blender and set the purée aside.

3. Heat the oil in a heavy medium saucepan over medium heat. Add the rice and cook, stirring constantly, until light golden brown, about 15 minutes. (This light toasting increases the flavor.) Pour the rice into the sieve and drain well.

4. Meanwhile, bring a small saucepan of lightly salted water to a boil. Add the fresh peas and cook until they are barely tender, about 5 minutes. (If using frozen peas, cook for 2 minutes.) Drain and rinse with cold water to stop their cooking. Set aside.

5. Return the rice mixture to the saucepan. Add the tomato purée, water, and salt. Bring to a boil over high heat. Reduce the heat to low and cover. Simmer until the rice is tender and the liquid is absorbed, about 20 minutes. Remove from the heat, add the peas, and let stand, covered, for 5 minutes. Serve immediately.

tamales de espinaca
spinach tamales

These tamales are excellent on their own, but I really love them as a side dish to Lamb Loin Chops in Garlicky Pasilla Sauce (page 128). They don't have any meat in them, so the lamb acts as a kind of accent. You will only need one or two tamales per serving with the lamb chops. Make the entire recipe, however, and freeze the remaining tamales for another meal. MAKES 12 TAMALES

12 dried corn husks

Masa (page 68)

1 cup packed baby spinach

2 plum (Roma) tomatoes, seeded and chopped

1 poblano chile, roasted, peeled (see page 22), and cut into ¼-inch-wide strips

½ cup Mexican crema or crème fraîche for serving

1. Soak the corn husks in a large bowl of warm water until pliable, about 20 minutes.

2. Drain the corn husks and pat dry with kitchen towels. Spread 2 or 3 tablespoons of Masa in a strip about 5 inches long and 3 inches wide in the center of a corn husk. Top with a few spinach leaves, a little chopped tomato, and a strip or two of chile. Fold over the sides of the husk to cover the filling with the Masa. Fold the top and bottom ends of the husk up and slip one end inside another to secure the husk closed. If you wish, tie the husk closed with kitchen twine. Repeat with the remaining husks, Masa, spinach, tomatoes, and chile. There may be some chile left over. (The tamales can be prepared up to 8 hours ahead, cooled and refrigerated.)

3. Bring water to a boil in a steamer. Arrange the tamales in the steamer and cover tightly. Cook until the Masa is firm, about 45 minutes to 1 hour. Check occasionally and add more boiling water to the steamer if needed.

4. Serve the hot tamales in their husks, or unwrap and cut each tamal into thirds. Pass the crema alongside.

salsas
sauces

salsa de chile de árbol
árbol chile sauce

The word *salsa* means "sauce" in Spanish but, just as in any cuisine, it comes in many different textures, consistencies, and flavors. Salsas fall into two basic categories: raw and cooked. This cooked salsa is a good accompaniment when you want to add heat to a dish. MAKES ABOUT 1 CUP

2 cups water

12 dried chiles de árbol, rinsed

½ teaspoon fine sea salt plus more for seasoning

4 ripe plum (Roma) tomatoes (1 pound)

½ white onion, quartered

4 large garlic cloves

1. Bring the water to a boil in a medium saucepan over medium heat. Add the chiles and ½ teaspoon salt and simmer until the chiles soften, about 5 minutes. Remove from the heat and let cool to room temperature.

2. Position a broiler rack 6 inches from the heat source and preheat the broiler. Place the tomatoes on a broiler pan and broil, turning occasionally, until the skin of the tomatoes is singed and splitting, about 5 minutes. Do not overcook the tomatoes or they will burst. Remove from the oven and let cool to the touch.

3. Reduce the oven temperature to 375°F. Put the onion and garlic on a baking sheet and roast until soft, about 20 minutes. Remove from the oven and let cool to room temperature.

4. Peel the tomatoes. Drain the chiles in a sieve over a bowl and reserve the cooking liquid. Put the tomatoes, onion, garlic, and chiles in a blender or food processor and pulse 4 or 5 times until the salsa is chunky, adding some of the reserved chile liquid if needed. Season to taste with salt. (The salsa can be made up to 5 days ahead, cooled, covered, and refrigerated.)

salsa de jitomate asado y chipotle
roasted tomato–chipotle sauce

Smoky chipotles and roasted tomatoes give this salsa a lot of character. Adjust the amount of chiles as you wish, but the sauce should be on the hot side. The chiles are quite spicy, so be careful not to touch them—lift them out of the can with the tip of a small sharp knife, or wear rubber gloves as a precaution—and use any adobo sauce that clings to the chiles.   MAKES ABOUT 2 CUPS

3 ripe plum (Roma) tomatoes (12 ounces)

7 canned chipotle chiles in adobo

½ teaspoon fine sea salt

½ cup water

1. Position a rack in the center of the oven and preheat the oven to 450°F. Place the tomatoes on a baking sheet and roast until the skins are split and dark brown, about 20 minutes. Remove from the oven. Let cool until easy to handle. Don't bother to peel the tomatoes, as the peels will be removed by straining later.

2. Put the tomatoes, chiles, salt, and water in a blender or food processor and process until smooth. Strain through a sieve into a bowl. (The salsa can be made up to 1 day ahead, covered and refrigerated.)

salsa de aguacate y tomatillo
avocado-tomatillo sauce

This smooth, pale green sauce is a fine accompaniment to seafood. Be sure that the avocado is properly ripe
(it should yield easily to a gentle squeeze), or it won't purée well.   MAKES ABOUT 2 CUPS

2 tomatillos

½ ripe avocado

½ cup packed fresh cilantro
leaves

¾ cup water

½ teaspoon fine sea salt

1. Remove the husks from the tomatillos. Rinse, drain, and coarsely chop the tomatillos. Peel, pit, and coarsely chop the avocado.

2. Put the tomatillos, avocado, cilantro leaves, water, and salt in a blender or food processor and process until smooth. Pour into a bowl. (The salsa can be made up to 1 day ahead, covered and refrigerated. Bring to room temperature before serving.)

salsa de molcajete
"mortar" salsa

Traditionally, this rustic salsa would be made in a *molcajete*, the lava rock mortar. Food ground in a molcajete acquires a
coarse texture, so if you make this in a food processor, try to keep the consistency bumpy and not smooth.
MAKES ABOUT 1 CUP

4 ripe plum (Roma) tomatoes

2 or 3 serrano chiles

Fine sea salt

1. Position the broiler rack 6 inches from the heat source and preheat the broiler. Place the tomatoes and chiles on a broiler pan and broil, turning occasionally, until the tomato skins are split and lightly scorched and the chile skins have turned olive green, about 7 minutes for the tomatoes and 5 minutes for the chiles. As the tomatoes and chiles are done, transfer them to a plate. Let cool to the touch. Leave the skins on the tomatoes, as they add extra flavor. For a milder salsa, remove the seeds from the chiles.

2. Put the tomatoes and chiles in a blender or food processor and pulse 3 or 4 times, just until the tomatoes have a coarse but semiliquid texture. Season to taste with salt. Transfer to a bowl. (The salsa is best served within a few hours of making, but it can be made up to 1 day ahead, covered and refrigerated. Bring to room temperature before serving.)

salsa de tomatillo asado
roasted tomatillo sauce

A short trip under the broiler tenderizes the tomatillos and mellows their flavor. If you prefer, fire up a charcoal or gas grill and grill the tomatillos and chiles until they change color. In that case, you'll add a touch of smokiness to the salsa, too. MAKES ABOUT 2 CUPS

1 pound tomatillos, husked and rinsed

2 serrano chiles (or more, if you like a hotter sauce)

½ cup packed fresh cilantro

¼ cup water

1 teaspoon fine sea salt

1. Position the broiler rack 6 inches from the heat source and preheat the broiler. Place the tomatillos and chiles on the broiler pan and broil, turning occasionally, until all sides of both have turned dark olive green, about 10 minutes. Do not overcook the tomatillos or they will burst. And there's no need to broil the chiles until they blacken and blister. Let cool to the touch. For a milder salsa, remove the seeds from the chiles.

2. Put the tomatillos, chiles, cilantro, water, and salt in a blender or food processor and process until smooth. Transfer to a bowl. (The salsa is best served within a few hours of making, but it can be made up to 1 day ahead, covered and refrigerated. Bring to room temperature before serving.)

puré de chile ancho o guajillo
ancho or guajillo chile purée

Two chile purées are the workhorses of ¡Salpicón!'s kitchen: ancho and guajillo. These chiles are only mildly hot, so they have a lot of versatility. When I want a spicier sauce, I use one of these as a base and add hotter chiles to it. Because the procedure is almost identical for either purée, I've included them both here. MAKES ABOUT 1 CUP

3 ancho chiles, seeded

3 cups boiling water

¼ white onion, coarsely chopped

1 garlic clove

Fine sea salt

1. Heat a heavy, preferably cast-iron medium skillet over medium-high heat. Add the chiles and cook, turning occasionally, until they become pliable and fragrant, about 1 minute. Do not overcook the chiles, or they will be bitter.

2. Put the chiles in a medium bowl and add the boiling water. Let stand until the chiles soften, about 20 minutes. Strain the chiles over a bowl, reserving the soaking water.

3. Put the softened chiles, ½ cup of the reserved soaking water, the onion, and garlic in a blender and process until smooth, adding more soaking water if needed to get a smooth purée. Strain through a fine-meshed sieve over a bowl. Season to taste with salt. (The purée can be made up to 3 days ahead, covered and refrigerated.)

Guajillo Chile Purée: Substitute 8 guajillo chiles for the ancho chiles, but allow 30 minutes for them to soften. Use about ¾ cup of the soaking water to purée the chiles.

salsa de chile ancho y miel
ancho-honey sauce

The ancho chile has a sweet flavor note, so matching it with honey is natural. I use this wonderful mixture as a sauce for Grilled Quail (page 139) and even as a glaze for Salmon with Fennel (page 98), but it would also be fantastic on barbecued spareribs or chicken from your grill. There's no need to use a fancy, distinctively flavored honey— a supermarket variety works well. MAKES ABOUT 1½ CUPS

1½ tablespoons canola oil

½ onion, finely chopped

1 cup Ancho Chile Purée (page 165)

½ cup honey

Pinch of ground cinnamon

Pinch of ground cloves

Fine sea salt

1. Heat the oil in a medium saucepan over medium heat. Add the onion and cook, stirring occasionally, until golden, about 4 minutes.

2. Stir in the Ancho Chile Purée, honey, cinnamon, and cloves. Season to taste with salt. Bring to a boil, reduce the heat to medium-low, and simmer, stirring occasionally, until slightly reduced, about 5 minutes. (The sauce can be made up to 2 weeks ahead, cooled, covered, and refrigerated. Bring to room temperature before using.)

salsa de cuatro chiles
four-chile sauce

This salsa takes a bit more work than the others, but you will be rewarded with a beautifully seasoned combination of four chiles with distinct heat levels and flavors. The moritas and chiles de árbol are quite spicy, so adjust their amount for a milder sauce, if you like. MAKES ABOUT 1 CUP

6 dried chiles de árbol

5 morita chiles, seeded

1 cup boiling water

½ cup Ancho Chile Purée (page 165)

½ cup Guajillo Chile Purée (page 165)

2 tablespoons canola oil

1. Put the chiles de árbol and moritas in a small bowl. Add the boiling water and let stand until the chiles soften, about 20 minutes. Strain in a sieve over a bowl, reserving the soaking liquid. Put the soaked chiles and ½ cup of the reserved soaking liquid into a blender and purée. Strain through a fine-meshed sieve over a bowl. Stir in the Ancho and Guajillo Chile Purées.

2. Heat the oil in a heavy, medium saucepan over medium heat. Add the chile purée mixture and reduce the heat to low. Simmer, stirring often, until the sauce is lightly thickened, about 20 minutes. (The sauce can be made up to 3 days ahead, cooled, covered, and refrigerated.) Serve at room temperature.

crema poblana
roasted poblano cream sauce

This sauce is so seductive, you may find yourself eating it with a spoon. Otherwise, you can serve it with chicken or pork chops.   MAKES ABOUT 2 CUPS

½ white onion, quartered

1 garlic clove, crushed

4 poblano chiles, roasted and peeled (see page 22)

1 cup half-and-half

1 tablespoon unsalted butter

½ cup heavy cream

Fine sea salt

1. Position a rack in the center of the oven and preheat the oven to 375°F. Place the onion and garlic on a baking sheet. Bake, checking occasionally to be sure that they aren't burning, until the onion is soft, about 20 minutes.

2. Put the onion, garlic, chiles, and half-and-half in a blender and purée. Strain through a sieve into a bowl.

3. Melt the butter in a medium saucepan, preferably nonstick, over medium heat. Add the chile purée and heavy cream and bring to a boil. Reduce the heat to medium-low and simmer until lightly thickened, about 5 minutes. Season to taste with salt. (The sauce can be made up to 2 hours ahead and stored at room temperature. Reheat to serve.) Serve hot.

aceite de cilantro
cilantro oil

When a dish needs a splash of color, a drizzle of bright green cilantro oil does the trick. You may be tempted to make a big batch, but it doesn't keep especially well, so a smaller batch is the way to go.   MAKES ABOUT ½ CUP

1 cup packed cilantro sprigs (about 35)

½ cup olive oil

Pinch of fine sea salt

1. Bring 4 cups water to a boil in a medium saucepan over high heat. Add the cilantro and blanch for 5 seconds. Drain. Plunge the cilantro into a bowl of ice water and let stand until cool. Drain again. Wrap the cilantro in paper towels and press gently to remove excess water.

2. Combine the cilantro, oil, and salt in a mini–food processor or a blender and process until smooth. Transfer to a bowl, cover, and let stand at room temperature for 4 hours. Strain through a very-fine-meshed sieve (or line a regular sieve with a damp, wrung-out cheesecloth). Funnel into a plastic squeeze bottle for easy serving. (The oil can be made up to 2 days ahead, covered and refrigerated. Bring to room temperature before serving.)

agua para marinar carnes
basic brine for meats

Brining has become an important technique for adding moisture to lean meats and poultry, and I especially like to brine pork chops before grilling to ensure juicy results. Brining is not a magic potion, however, and should be used only with very lean cuts with little intramuscular fat—it is not needed with fatty cuts like pork shoulder or lamb shanks. And don't let the meat stand too long in the brine, or it will toughen. The brine works best when it is ice-cold, so try to chill it overnight or in a bowl of ice water before using.   MAKES 8 CUPS

8 cups water

½ cup kosher salt

½ cup sugar

¼ cup juniper berries

¼ cup black peppercorns

2 tablespoons fennel seeds

2 tablespoons coriander seeds

1. Bring the water, salt, sugar, juniper berries, peppercorns, fennel, and coriander to a boil in a medium saucepan over high heat, stirring often to dissolve the salt and sugar. Reduce the heat to low and simmer for 3 minutes to bring out the flavors of the spices.

2. Pour into a bowl and let cool until tepid. Place the bowl in a larger bowl of ice water or refrigerate it until chilled. (The brine can be made up to 1 day ahead, covered and refrigerated.)

salsa de mango
mango sauce

This golden orange sauce not only acts as a garnish to fruit pastries (especially my Pear and Mango Tartlets on page 180), but is also a great sauce for ice cream. The mango itself must be perfectly ripe—they're ready when they smell like sweet perfume and have a few tiny brown spots on the skin. **MAKES ABOUT 1½ CUPS**

1 large, ripe mango, peeled and pitted (see page 41)

¾ cup Simple Syrup (recipe follows)

1. Coarsely chop the mango flesh.

2. Put the mango flesh and Simple Syrup in a blender and process until smooth. Strain through a sieve into a bowl. (The mango sauce can be prepared up to 2 days ahead, covered and refrigerated.) Serve at room temperature.

Simple Syrup: Bring 1 cup water and 1 cup sugar to a full boil in a small saucepan over high heat, stirring constantly to help dissolve the sugar. Reduce the heat to low and simmer for 1 minute. Remove from the heat and let cool completely. Transfer to a covered glass container and refrigerate indefinitely.

postres
desserts

pasteles de chocolate con crema de café
warm chocolate-espresso cakes with coffee bean sauce

Not too long ago, individual warm chocolate cakes with soft centers were an unusual dessert. Now they are almost required items on a successful restaurant's menu, and this is how we make them, packed with dark-roasted coffee. While the coffee supplies its own flavor, it also intensifies the chocolate. After all, both ingredients are created from tropical beans. MAKES 6 SERVINGS

COFFEE BEAN SAUCE

1 cup whole milk

½ cup coarsely crushed dark-roasted coffee beans such as French or Italian roast

1 large egg yolk

2 tablespoons sugar

CHOCOLATE CAKES

10 tablespoons (1¼ sticks) unsalted butter at room temperature

4 ounces bittersweet chocolate, coarsely chopped

3 large eggs

3 large egg yolks

¾ cup confectioners' sugar, sifted, plus more for dusting

½ cup cake flour, sifted

¼ cup freshly brewed espresso, or 1¼ teaspoons instant espresso powder dissolved in ¼ cup boiling water

Vanilla ice cream for serving

Fresh mint sprigs for garnish

1. At least 6 hours before serving, make the sauce: Heat the milk and coffee beans in a small saucepan over medium heat until tiny bubbles appear around the edges of the milk, about 4 minutes. Remove from the heat and cover the saucepan. Let stand for 10 minutes.

2. Whisk the egg yolk and sugar in a small bowl until thick and pale yellow. Gradually whisk about half of the hot milk mixture into the yolk mixture, then whisk this into the saucepan. Cook over low heat, stirring constantly with a wooden spatula, until the sauce registers 185°F on an instant-read thermometer and it is thick enough to coat the spatula (if you run your finger down the sauce on the spatula, it will cut a swath), about 4 minutes. Strain through a sieve into a bowl, pressing hard on the beans. Press a piece of plastic wrap directly onto the surface of the coffee sauce. Let cool, then refrigerate for at least 6 hours or overnight to mellow the flavors.

3. To make the cakes: Generously butter six 3- to 4-inch-diameter ramekins. Combine the butter and chocolate in a double boiler. Melt over barely simmering water, stirring occasionally, until smooth. Remove from the heat and set aside.

4. Whisk the eggs and egg yolks in a medium bowl. Gradually whisk in the ¾ cup confectioners' sugar until smooth. Whisk the sugar mixture into the melted chocolate mixture. Add the flour and

espresso and mix until the batter is smooth. Spoon into the ramekins and smooth the tops. Refrigerate for at least 1 hour or up to 8 hours.

5. Position a rack in the center of the oven and preheat the oven to 325°F. Transfer the ramekins to a large baking sheet. Bake until the edges are set but the center looks slightly underbaked, 18 to 21 minutes. Do not overbake, or you will lose the ooze effect and end up with cupcakes. Let stand in the ramekins for 2 minutes.

6. To serve, run a dull knife around the inside of the ramekins. Invert and unmold the cakes onto each of 6 dessert plates. Add a small scoop of ice cream to each. Dust the tops with confectioners' sugar and spoon some of the sauce around each cake. Garnish with a mint sprig and serve at once.

WINE NOTES

An excellent match for dark chocolate is the Grenache-based dessert wine known as Banyuls from the southern Rhône valley. Excellent producers are Dr. Parcé, Chapoutier, and Helyos.

trufas de tequila
tequila truffles

If you asked ¡Salpicón!'s clientele about their favorite dessert, chocolate would tie with an after-dinner drink. After sipping tequila while nibbling at a chocolate dessert, I decided that the two are actually a good pair, playing off each other's strengths. For these silky truffles, a mild silver tequila is best, as the flavor of a richer tequila could fight the chocolate. If you want to save the tequila for drinking on its own, flavor the truffles with the more traditional orange or coffee liqueur. MAKES ABOUT 4 DOZEN TRUFFLES

¾ cup heavy cream

1 vanilla bean, split lengthwise

5 large egg yolks

12 ounces semisweet chocolate, finely chopped (see Note)

½ cup (1 stick) unsalted butter, cut into small cubes, at room temperature

¼ cup silver tequila

About 2 cups unsweetened cocoa powder for rolling the truffles

1. Bring the cream and vanilla bean to a simmer in a medium saucepan over medium heat. Remove from the heat, cover, and let stand for 10 minutes. Remove the bean from the cream and use the tip of a small knife to scrape the vanilla bean pulp back into the cream. Discard the vanilla bean.

2. Whisk the yolks in a medium bowl. Gradually whisk about ¼ cup of the hot cream into the yolks, then whisk this mixture back into the saucepan.

3. Combine the chocolate and butter in a medium bowl. Pour the hot cream mixture over the chocolate. Let stand until the chocolate softens, about 5 minutes. Whisk until smooth. Whisk in the tequila. Cover and refrigerate until firm, at least 4 hours.

4. Using a melon baller, scoop up the truffle mixture and roll between your palms into a ball. Repeat to make about 50 truffles. Spread the cocoa in a shallow dish. Roll the truffles in the cocoa to coat. Cover and refrigerate until ready to serve, up to 5 days. Remove from the refrigerator about 1 hour before serving.

NOTE: Today's chocolate-lover has a huge range of chocolates to choose from. Many brands are now labeled with their cacao content. (Cacao is the processed but unsweetened pulp of the bean.) The higher the amount of cacao, the more bitter the chocolate. As the tequila in this recipe also has a slightly bitter flavor, it needs to be balanced by a relatively sweet chocolate. When it comes to chocolate, the terms "bittersweet" and "semisweet" are not always helpful, as there is no standard for the amount of sugar—one manufacturer's bittersweet could be as sweet as another's semisweet. For these truffles, choose a semisweet chocolate with a cacao content of about 55%. The percentages are sometimes marked on the label, if not on the front, then on the back. If not, just avoid the ones that are labeled with cacao contents of above 60%, or your truffles could be too bitter.

WINE NOTES
I like to pair these chocolate delights with añejo tequila. Excellent ones are produced by Herradura, Don Julio, and Corazón.

pastel tres leches
"three milks" cake

Three (actually six) dairy products combine to make this luscious dessert. It seems to be a Nicaraguan invention but is now embraced throughout the Hispanic world. In Mexico this cake is usually served on birthdays. Make it at least a few hours before serving so the cake can soak up every drop of the "three milks" infusion. The cake is especially nice when served with a fruit purée—raspberry, mango, or prickly pear are equally delicious. MAKES 8 SERVINGS

CAKE

1¾ cups cake flour

1½ teaspoons baking powder

¼ teaspoon fine sea salt

10 tablespoons (1¼ sticks) unsalted butter at room temperature

1¼ cups granulated sugar

4 large eggs, separated

¾ cup whole milk

"THREE MILKS" SOAKING LIQUID

One 12-ounce can evaporated milk

One 14-ounce can sweetened condensed milk

½ cup half-and-half

Grated zest of 3 oranges

ICING

2 cups heavy cream

½ cup confectioners' sugar

1. To make the cake: Position a rack in the center of the oven and preheat the oven to 350°F. Lightly butter a 9-inch-round cake pan that is 2 inches deep, then line the bottom of the pan with a round of waxed paper and butter the paper. Dust the inside with flour and tap out the excess.

2. Sift the flour, baking powder, and salt together into a medium bowl. Beat the butter and sugar together with an electric mixer on high speed until light and fluffy, about 3 minutes. One at a time, add the egg yolks, beating well after each addition. Reduce the mixer speed to low. Add the flour mixture in 3 increments, alternating with 2 increments of milk, scraping down the sides of the bowl as needed.

3. Using clean beaters, beat the egg whites in a large bowl until stiff peaks form. Stir one-fourth of the beaten whites into the batter, then fold in the rest with a rubber spatula. Spread evenly in the prepared pan.

4. Bake until a toothpick inserted in the center of the cake comes out clean, about 35 minutes. Let cool on a wire rack for 10 minutes. Unmold the cake onto the rack and peel off the waxed paper. Let cool completely.

5. To make the "three milks" soaking liquid: Whisk the evaporated and condensed milks, half-and-half, and orange zest in a medium bowl until combined.

Using a long, serrated knife, trim off the top crust from the cake. Return the cake to the pan, top side down. Slowly spoon the three-milks mixture over the cake, letting each addition soak in before adding more. Repeat until all of the milk mixture is absorbed.

6. To make the icing: Beat the cream and confectioners' sugar with an electric mixer on high speed in a chilled medium bowl until stiff. Invert the cake onto a cake stand or serving platter. Spread the icing over the top and sides of the cake. Refrigerate until the cake is chilled, at least 1 hour or overnight. Serve chilled.

WINE NOTES

An excellent pairing for this cake is Yalumba's Muscat Victoria Museum Release from Australia. Also good is Essencia Orange Muscat by Quady. Both of these wines pick up the fruit flavors in the cake.

arroz con leche caramelizado
rice pudding brûlée

When I was growing up, this dessert showed up often at the dinner table. Today, a spoonful of this comforting pudding brings back homey memories. The caramelized sugar topping makes it a bit more contemporary, but it is still the classic that I love. For the best results with the topping, serve the puddings in 5-inch-wide crème brûlée dishes, and use a handheld kitchen torch for the caramelizing. Otherwise, use the widest ramekins or custard dishes you have, and caramelize them under the broiler. MAKES 6 SERVINGS

2 cups water

One 1-inch piece cinnamon stick

One 4-inch strip orange zest, removed with a vegetable peeler

1 cup long-grain rice

4 cups whole milk

¾ cup plus 6 teaspoons sugar

Pinch of salt

1 cup half-and-half

2 large egg yolks, beaten

½ cup raisins

Fresh mint sprigs for garnish

1. Bring the water, cinnamon, and orange zest to a boil in a medium saucepan over medium heat. Place the rice in a sieve and rinse under cold running water. Drain and add to the saucepan. Reduce the heat to medium-low and simmer, uncovered, stirring occasionally, until the water is evaporated (the rice will not be completely cooked), about 8 minutes.

2. Stir in the milk, the ¾ cup sugar, and the salt. Bring to a simmer over medium-high heat. Return the heat to medium-low and simmer, uncovered, stirring often, until the rice is tender, about 20 minutes. Remove from the heat and let cool to room temperature.

3. Just before serving, stir the half-and-half, egg yolks, and raisins into the rice mixture. Spoon into 6 crème brûlée dishes. Sprinkle the top of each pudding evenly with 1 teaspoon sugar. To create the brûlée topping, wave the flame of a handheld kitchen torch about 1 inch above the sugar until the sugar melts and caramelizes. Serve immediately, garnished with the mint.

WINE NOTES

A full-bodied, late-harvest dessert wine would be excellent. Choose Muscat de Beaumes-de-Venise from France (Jaboulet or Chapoutier), Muscat Ottonel of Furmint from Austria (Kracher or Heidi Schröck), or ice wine from Canada (Inniskillin) or Washington State (Chateau Ste. Michelle).

flan de naranja
orange-flavored flan

Creamy, silken flan in caramel sauce is perhaps the classic Mexican dessert. To give it that amazingly smooth texture, it is important to cook the custards at low heat in a covered hot-water bath—the trapped steam helps to cook the flans from the top, making them set sooner and preventing overcooking, which causes curdling. My version adds another layer of flavor with orange zest, but I have included a vanilla variation for purists.

MAKES 4 SERVINGS

1½ cups sugar

½ cup water

1 cup whole milk

1 cup half-and-half

Grated zest of 3 oranges

4 large eggs at room temperature

1. Place four 3- to 4-inch ramekins by the stove. Bring 1 cup of the sugar and the water to a boil in a small saucepan over high heat, stirring just until the sugar dissolves. Cook without stirring but occasionally swirling the pan by the handle, until dark amber, about 8 minutes. Immediately (and carefully) pour hot caramel into each ramekin, swirling it to coat the bottom and part way up the sides. Set aside.

2. Preheat oven to 325°F. Cook the milk, half-and-half, the remaining ½ cup sugar, and the orange zest in a medium saucepan over medium-high heat, stirring frequently, until small bubbles form around the edges of the milk. Remove from the heat. Whisk the eggs in a medium bowl until well combined. Gradually whisk in the hot milk mixture. Strain the custard through a fine-meshed sieve into a 4-cup liquid measuring cup. Pour equal amounts of the custard into the ramekins.

3. Place the ramekins in a roasting pan. Add boiling water to come halfway up the sides of the ramekins. Cover the pan with aluminum foil. Bake until the custards are barely set around the edges (the centers will still jiggle when shaken gently), about 25 minutes. Remove the ramekins from the pan. Let cool to room temperature. Cover each ramekin with plastic wrap and refrigerate until chilled, at least 4 hours or up to 2 days.

4. To serve, run a small knife around the edges of each ramekin. Unmold each onto a dessert plate. Serve chilled.

VANILLA FLANS: Substitute 1 vanilla bean for the orange zest. Using a small knife, split the bean lengthwise, then use the tip of the knife to scrape the vanilla seeds from the bean into the saucepan; add the empty bean, too. Discard the vanilla bean after straining, or rinse, dry, and immerse it in granulated sugar to scent the sugar for making desserts.

WINE NOTES
One of the classic food-and-wine pairings is caramel and tawny port. Try a ten-year tawny produced by Taylor Fladgate or Fonseca.

tartaletas de pera y mango
pear and mango tartlets

Another favorite dessert at ¡Salpicón!, these attractive tartlets celebrate the perfumed sweetness of ripe mangos—they appear in the filling, as a sauce, and as a "tuile" garnish (a *tuile* is usually a very thin, crisp cookie, but they can be fabricated by oven-drying sliced fruit, too). Pears, however, which break down slightly to give the filling body as well as flavor, play a role here as well. You will need eight 3-inch tartlet pans with removable bottoms for these.   **MAKES 8 TARTLETS**

MANGO "TUILES"

1 firm, ripe mango, peeled and pitted (see page 41)

¼ cup Simple Syrup (page 171)

PASTRY DOUGH

2 cups all-purpose flour

⅔ cup granulated sugar

1 tablespoon baking powder

¼ teaspoon fine sea salt

¾ cup (1½ sticks) unsalted butter, cut into ½-inch cubes, at room temperature

½ cup heavy cream, chilled

FILLING

2 tablespoons unsalted butter

1 large, ripe mango, peeled, pitted, and diced (page 41)

2 ripe Anjou pears, peeled, cored, and diced

¼ cup granulated sugar

Seeds from 1 vanilla bean

ALMOND TOPPING

1 cup chopped natural almonds

⅓ cup natural ("raw") sugar

¼ cup all-purpose flour

2 tablespoons cold unsalted butter, cut into ¼-inch cubes

Mango Sauce (page 171) for serving

Vanilla ice cream for serving

Fresh mint sprigs for garnish

1. To make the mango "tuiles": Position a rack in the center of the oven and preheat the oven to 200°F. Line a baking sheet with a silicone liner. Cut the peeled and pitted mango with a mandolin into ¹⁄₁₆-inch lengthwise slices. Arrange the slices on the baking sheet and brush with Simple Syrup (you may have some leftover syrup). Bake until the mango slices are dry and lightly golden, about 45 minutes. Transfer the mango "tuiles" to a cake rack to cool completely. (The "tuiles" can be made up to 1 day ahead and stored in an airtight container at room temperature.)

2. To make the pastry dough: Combine the flour, sugar, baking powder, and salt in a medium bowl. Stir with a whisk to blend. Add the butter. Using an electric mixer on low speed, mix until the mixture looks crumbly. Add the heavy cream and mix just

until the dough comes together. Gather up into a disk, wrap in plastic wrap, and refrigerate for at least 1 hour or up to 24 hours. (If the dough is well chilled, let it stand at room temperature for 10 minutes to soften slightly before rolling out.)

3. To make the filling: Melt the butter in a medium saucepan over medium heat. Add the diced mango, pears, sugar, and vanilla seeds. Bring to a boil, stirring frequently. Reduce the heat to medium-low and cook, stirring often, until it has a jamlike consistency, about 20 minutes. Transfer to a bowl and let cool completely.

4. To make the topping: Combine the almonds, natural sugar, flour, and butter in a small bowl. Using your fingertips, work the ingredients together until combined and crumbly.

5. Generously butter eight 3-inch tartlet pans with removable bottoms. Cut the chilled dough into 8 equal pieces. Working with one piece at a time, roll the dough into a 4-inch round. Fit the dough into a tartlet pan, being sure the dough is tucked into the corners. Using a sharp knife, trim off the excess dough. Place the pan on a large baking sheet. Repeat with the remaining dough. Refrigerate until the pastry shells are chilled, about 30 minutes.

6. Position a rack in the bottom third of the oven and preheat the oven to 375°F.

7. Fill each tartlet with an equal amount of the filling and sprinkle with a generous amount of the almond topping. Bake until the edges of the pastry are golden brown, about 25 minutes. Remove from the oven and let stand for 5 minutes.

8. To serve, spoon a few tablespoons of the Mango Sauce in the center of each of 8 dessert plates. Using a kitchen towel to protect your hands, unmold the tartlets and place one in the center of each plate. Top each with a scoop of ice cream, a "tuile," and a mint sprig. Serve immediately.

WINE NOTES
Late-harvest-style dessert wines from different countries and regions work well with the fruit and nuts in these tartlets. From Bordeaux, look for Sauternes and Barsacs. Excellent producers are Château Rieussec and Château Suduiraut. In the Loire Valley, dessert wines are produced from the Chenin Blanc grape, and Domaine des Baumard is the ruler here. Kracher from Austria makes phenomenal dessert wines from the native Austrian grapes Weissburgunder and Welschriesling.

trio de piña
pineapple three ways

The "three ways" in the title are a pineapple sorbet, "tuiles" (thin slices of pineapple crisped in the oven), and caramelized pineapple slices. You'll get a wonderful variety of textures, temperatures, and flavors from two ripe pineapples. You will have more pineapple sorbet than you need, but I just can't see why one would want to make a small amount of something that is so delicious. **MAKES 6 SERVINGS**

2 ripe pineapples, peeled

PINEAPPLE "TUILES"
¼ cup Simple Syrup (page 171)

CARMELIZED PINEAPPLE
½ cup (1 stick) unsalted butter, cut into 8 slices
6 cups water
1¼ cups packed light brown sugar
Seeds from 1 vanilla bean

SORBET
1 cup Simple Syrup (page 171)
2 tablespoons corn syrup

Confectioners' sugar for dusting
Fresh mint sprigs for garnish

1. Cut one pineapple in half crosswise. With a mandolin, cut six 1/16-inch-thick slices lengthwise from the sides of one pineapple half; set aside for the "tuiles." Core the other pineapple half, cut crosswise into 6 rings, and set aside for the caramelized pineapple. Core the remaining pineapple, coarsely chop, and set aside for the sorbet.

2. To make the pineapple "tuiles": Position a rack in the center of the oven and preheat the oven to 200°F. Line a baking sheet with a silicone liner. Arrange the lengthwise pineapple slices on the baking sheet and brush with the ¼ cup Simple Syrup (you may have some leftover syrup). Bake until the pineapple is dry and lightly golden, about 45 minutes. Transfer the pineapple "tuiles" to a wire rack to cool completely.

3. To make the caramelized pineapple: Layer the pineapple rings, butter, water, brown sugar, and vanilla seeds in a large saucepan. Bring to a boil over high heat, shaking the pan to help dissolve the brown sugar. Reduce the heat to low and simmer, uncovered, until the pineapple is tender but not falling apart, and the liquid has reduced to a thick syrup, about 2½ hours. If the pineapple is tender before the syrup is thick, remove the pineapple with a slotted spoon to a plate, then boil the syrup until thickened. Remove from the heat and let cool to warm. (The pineapple and its syrup can be made up to 1 day ahead, cooled, covered, and refrigerated. Reheat gently before serving.)

4. To make the sorbet: Purée the chopped pineapple in a blender. Strain through a sieve into a bowl. Stir in the 1 cup Simple Syrup and the corn syrup. Cover and refrigerate until chilled, about 2 hours. Freeze in an ice cream maker according to the manufacturer's directions. Transfer to an airtight container and freeze for at least 2 hours before serving. (The sorbet can be frozen for up to 2 days.)

5. To serve, place a caramelized pineapple and some of its syrup on each of 6 plates. Place a scoop of sorbet in the center of each ring, then stand a pineapple "tuile" in the sorbet. Freeze any remaining sorbet. Sift confectioners' sugar over the top and garnish with a mint sprig. Serve immediately.

WINE NOTES
Any botrytis-affected wine works well with this dish. Sauternes and Barsacs from France, Weissburgunders and Welschrieslings from Austria, and late-harvest "stickies" from Australia are very friendly with pineapple.

nieve de tuna con galletas de lima
prickly pear sorbet in lime tuiles

The prickly pear is the fruit of an edible cactus. The bright red or magenta fruit makes a sorbet that is as beautiful as it is delicious. I usually serve the sorbet by itself, but for a special occasion, scoop it into crisp lime tuiles. Without the cookies, you could serve it at a formal dinner party as a palate cleanser between courses. **MAKES 8 SERVINGS**

SORBET

3 pounds ripe prickly pears

¾ cup sugar

⅓ cup corn syrup

LIME TUILES

1 large egg white

5 tablespoons sugar

3 tablespoons unsalted butter, melted

⅓ cup all-purpose flour

Grated zest of 1 lime

1. To make the sorbet: Trim the top and bottom of each pear with a sharp knife. Make a lengthwise cut, then peel off the thick skin. Coarsely chop the flesh.

2. Purée the prickly pear flesh in a blender. Strain through a fine-meshed sieve into a bowl to remove the seeds. Stir in the sugar and corn syrup. Cover and refrigerate until chilled, about 2 hours. Freeze in an ice cream maker according to the manufacturer's directions. Transfer to an airtight container and freeze for at least 2 hours before serving. (The sorbet can be frozen for up to 2 days.)

3. To make the tuiles: Beat the egg white in a medium bowl with an electric mixer on high speed until soft peaks form. One tablespoon at a time, beat in the sugar until the whites are stiff and shiny. Fold in the butter, then the flour and zest. Let stand to thicken slightly, about 5 minutes.

4. Position racks in the center and upper third of the oven and preheat the oven to 325°F. Line 2 heavy 18-by-12-inch baking sheets with parchment paper or silicone mats. Invert 8 custard cups on a work surface near the stove.

5. Spoon 1 tablespoon of the batter onto a baking sheet. Using a small offset metal spatula, spread the batter into a very thin 6-inch round. Repeat, spacing the batter about 4 inches apart, to make

2 tuiles per baking sheet. Bake until the tuiles are completely golden brown, about 8 minutes. Do not underbake.

6. Remove the baking sheets from the oven and let stand until the cookies are cool enough to remove from the baking sheet, about 45 seconds. Using a metal spatula and working quickly, remove a warm, flexible cookie from the baking sheet and drape it over a custard cup. Use your hands to gently mold the tuile to the shape of the cup. As the tuiles cool, they will harden and take on the cup's form. If the tuiles harden on the baking sheet, return the baking sheet to the oven to warm and soften them, then transfer them to the cups. Let stand until the tuiles are cooled and crisp. Carefully remove them from the cups. (The tuiles can be made up to 1 day ahead and stored in an airtight container.) Repeat with the remaining batter, being sure to cool the baking sheets (and silicone mats, if using).

7. To serve, place each tuile on a dessert plate and fill with scoops of the sorbet. Serve immediately.

WINE NOTES

This is a refreshing sorbet, and the wine should also be light but palate cleansing. Moscato d'Asti from the Piedmont region of Italy is an excellent pairing. Great producers are Vietti, Ceretto, and Saracco.

JB Prince
36 East 31st Street
New York, NY 10016
1-800-473-0577
www.jbprince.com

Entremets molds, turning slicers, mandolins, and other professional cooking tools.

D'Artagnan
280 Wilson Avenue
Newark, NJ 07105
1-800-327-8246 x0
www.dartagnan.com

Mail-order source for such specialty meat products as duck legs and duck fat.

MexGrocer.com
4060 Morena Blvd., Suite C
San Diego, CA 92117
1-877-463-9476
www.mexgrocer.com

One-stop shopping for nonperishable Mexican groceries: corn husks for tamales, masa, piloncillo, dried chiles, and more.

Penzeys Spices
19300 Janacek Court
Brookfield, WI 53045
1-800-741-7787
www.penzeys.com

Excellent place to buy dried chiles, both whole and ground. Order online, or check out its Web site to find a retail store near you.

Burns Farms
1345 Bay Lake Loop
Groveland, FL 34736
1-352-429-4048

Excellent source for high-quality huitlacoche.

index

Aceite de cilantro, 169
Agua para marinar carnes, 170
Almonds
    Almond Mole, 133
    Pear and Mango Tartlets, 180–81
Arroz a la poblana, 150
Arroz blanco, 150
Arroz con leche caramelizado, 178
Arroz mexicano, 153
Avocados
    Avocado-Habanero Sauce, 43
    Avocado Mousse, 38
    Avocado-Tomatillo Sauce, 162
    buying, 21
    Chilled Avocado and Crab Soup, 78
    "Chopped" Guacamole, 48
    Grapefruit-Corn Salsa, 97
    storing, 21
    Stuffed Poblano Chiles with Avocado and Potatoes, 55

Bacon
    Bacon-Wrapped Sea Scallops, 30
    Lentil Soup, 74
    Pinto Beans with Bacon and Poblano Chiles, 149
Beans
    Black Bean and Chihuahua Cheese Tamales, 68
    Black Bean and Habanero Sauce, 120
    Black Bean Purée, 68
    Black Bean Sauce, 51
    buying, 21
    cooking, 21
    Grilled Octopus Salad, 82
    Morita Bean Purée, 30
    Pinto Beans with Bacon and Poblano Chiles, 149
    Pinto Beans with Chihuahua Cheese and Chiles, 149
    soaking, 21
Beef
    Beef in Green Mole, 116
    Beef Tenderloin Filets with Shiitakes in Morita Chile
      and Tomatillo Sauce, 119
    Cold Marinated Beef Brisket, 59
Beets
    Beet and Onion Strings, 44
    Beet Juice, 44
    Christmas Eve Salad, 90
Bread, Garlic, 111
Brine, Basic, for Meats, 170

Cactus. *See* Nopales; Prickly pears
Cakes
    "Three Milks" Cake, 176
    Warm Chocolate-Espresso Cakes with Coffee Bean
      Sauce, 174
Calamari
    Seafood Stew, 109–10

Caldo de mariscos, 109–10
Callos de hacha con tocino, 30
Camarones al carbón con dos salsas, 41
Carne en mole verde, 116
Cheese
    Black Bean and Chihuahua Cheese Tamales, 68
    Cheese and Chile Tamales, 70
    Lentil Soup, 74
    Mexican-style, 21
    Oysters in Chipotle Cream Sauce, 112
    Pinto Beans with Chihuahua Cheese and Chiles, 149
    Potato Cakes with Aged Mexican Cheese, 146
    Scalloped Potatoes, 146
    Spinach Salad with Chipotle-Honey Dressing, 86
    Squash Blossoms Stuffed with Goat Cheese, 56
    Stuffed Chilaca Chiles, 105
    Stuffed Jalapeños with Chihuahua Cheese, 51
Chicken
    Baby Chickens with Guajillo Sauce, 130
    Chicken Breasts in Ginger Mole, 129
Chiles
    Almond Mole, 133
    Ancho or Guajillo Chile Purée, 165
    Ancho-Chile Sauce, 123
    Ancho-Glazed Salmon with Fennel, 98
    Ancho-Honey Sauce, 166
    Árbol Chile Sauce, 158
    Avocado-Habanero Sauce, 43
    Baby Chickens with Guajillo Sauce, 130
    Black Bean and Chihuahua Cheese Tamales, 68
    Black Bean and Habanero Sauce, 120
    canned and bottled, 25
    Cheese and Chile Tamales, 70
    Chile Cream, 47
    Chile Oil, 139
    Chipotle-Honey Dressing, 86
    Chipotle Seafood Sauce, 33
    Chipotle Vinaigrette, 59
    Four-Chile Sauce, 166
    Ginger Mole, 129
    ground, 23
    Guajillo Chile Seasoning, 109
    heat of, 22
    Morita Bean Purée, 30
    Morita Chile and Tomatillo Sauce, 119
    Oysters in Chipotle Cream Sauce, 112
    Pasilla Sauce, 128
    Pasilla-Tomatillo Sauce, 127
    Pinto Beans with Bacon and Poblano Chiles, 149
    Pinto Beans with Chihuahua Cheese and Chiles, 149
    Red Mole Sauce, 124
    Rice with Poblano Chiles, 150
    Roasted Poblano Cream Sauce, 169
    Roasted Poblano Strips with Cream, 142
    Roasted Tomato–Chipotle Sauce, 161
    roasting fresh, 22
    Shredded Pork with Roasted Tomatoes and Chipotle
      Chiles, 60
    soaking dried, 23

Stuffed Chilaca Chiles, 105
Stuffed Jalapeños with Chihuahua Cheese, 51
Stuffed Poblano Chiles with Avocado and Potatoes, 55
toasting dried, 23
varieties of, 22–23
wine and, 18
Zucchini and Chipotle Tamales, 69
Chimichurri, Spicy, 62
Chocolate
    cacao content of, 175
    Red Mole Sauce, 124
    Tequila Truffles, 175
    Warm Chocolate-Espresso Cakes with Coffee Bean
      Sauce, 174
Chorizo, Mexican
    Potatoes with Chorizo, 145
    substitution for, 25
Christmas Eve Salad, 90
Chuleta de puerco en salsa de chile ancho, 123
*Chuleta de ternera en salsa de frijoles negros y
    habanero*, 120
Chuletas de borrego en salsa de pasilla, 128
Cilantro
    chopping, 25
    Cilantro Oil, 169
    storing, 25
Clams
    Seafood Stew, 109–10
Codornices en salsa de chile ancho y miel, 139
Coffee Bean Sauce, Warm Chocolate-Espresso Cakes
    with, 174
Corn
    Corn Relish, 56
    Corn Soup with Star Anise, 81
    Grapefruit-Corn Salsa, 97
    Green Salsa, 34
    Grilled Octopus Salad, 82
    Roasted Poblano Strips with Cream, 142
Costillitas de borrego con corteza de pepitas, 127
Crab
    Chilled Avocado and Crab Soup, 78
    Chipotle Seafood Sauce, 33
    Crab Cakes with Avocado-Habanero Sauce, 43–44
    Grilled Cactus and Seafood Napoleons with Chipotle
      Cream, 33
    Soft-Shell Crabs with Sweet Garlic Sauce, 106
Crema, 25
Crema poblano, 169
Cucumber Sorbet, Spicy, Mexican-Style Gazpacho with, 77

Desserts
    Orange-Flavored Flan, 179
    Pear and Mango Tartlets, 180–81
    Pineapple Three Ways, 183
    Prickly Pear Sorbet in Lime Tuiles, 184
    Rice Pudding Brûlée, 178
    Tequila Truffles, 175
    "Three Milks" Cake, 176

Vanilla Flan, 179
Warm Chocolate-Espresso Cakes with Coffee Bean
    Sauce, 174
Duck
    Duck Leg Confit with Pomegranate, 135–36
    Duck Two Ways in Ancho-Almond Sauce, 133–34

Empanadas de picadillo, 62–63
Ensalada de espinaca con aderezo de chipotle y miel, 86
Ensalada de nochebuena, 90
Ensalada de nopales, 89
Ensalada de pulpo, 82
Ensalada de verdolagas, 85

Fennel, Ancho-Glazed Salmon with, 98
*Filetes de res con shiitakes en salsa de morita y
    tomatillo*, 119
Fish
    Ancho-Glazed Salmon with Fennel, 98
    Black Sea Bass with Mushrooms and Two Sauces, 101
    Fish Fillets Veracruz-Style, 102
    Fish in Caper Sauce with Stuffed Chilaca Chiles, 105
    Fish Seviche, 37
    Fish Stock, 109
    Halibut in Parchment with Tequila, 94
    Salmon with Red Papaya–Tequila Sauce, 97
    Seafood Stew, 109–10
    Tequila-Cured Salmon Tartare with Tuna, 47
Flan de naranja, 179
Flans
    Orange-Flavored Flan, 179
    Vanilla Flans, 179
Flores de calabaza con queso de cabra, 56
Four-Chile Sauce, 166
Frijoles charros, 149
Frijoles maneados, 149

Garlic
    Garlic Bread, 111
    Roasted Garlic Cloves, 55
    Sweet Garlic Sauce, 106
Gazpacho, Mexican-Style, with Spicy Cucumber Sorbet, 77
Gazpacho mexicano con nieve de pepino y serrano, 77
Ginger Mole, 129
Grapefruit
    Grapefruit-Corn Salsa, 97
    peeling and segmenting, 90
Grouper
    Fish Fillets Veracruz-Style, 102
    Fish in Caper Sauce with Stuffed Chilaca Chiles, 105
Guacamole, "Chopped," 48
Guacamole picado, 48

Halibut in Parchment with Tequila, 94

Jaibas al mojo de ajo, 106
Jalapeños rellenos de queso chihuahua, 51

Jícama
    buying, 25
    Christmas Eve Salad, 90
    Grilled Portobellos with Chipotle Sauce, 52

Lamb
    Baby Racks of Lamb with a Pumpkin-Seed Crust, 127
    Lamb Loin Chops in Garlicky Pasilla Sauce, 128
    Lamb Shanks in Oxacan Red Mole Sauce, 124–25
Langostinos con salsa verde cruda, 34
Langoustines with "Raw" Green Salsa, 34
Lentil Soup, 74
Limes
    Fish Seviche, 37
    Lime-Oregano Dressing, 82
    Lime Tuiles, 184
    Lobster Seviche with Oranges and Serranos, 38

Mahi mahi
    Fish Fillets Veracruz-Style, 102
    Fish in Caper Sauce with Stuffed Chilaca Chiles, 105
Mangoes
    Grilled Shrimp with Two Sauces, 41
    Mango Sauce, 171
    Mango "Tuiles," 180
    Pear and Mango Tartlets, 180–81
    peeling and pitting, 41
Masa, 67, 68
Mejillones al cilantro con vino blanco y chiles serranos, 111
Mexican Rice, 153
Mexican-Style Gazpacho with Spicy Cucumber Sorbet, 77
Mixiote de borrego en mole coloradito, 124–25
Mole
    Almond Mole, 133
    Ginger Mole, 129
    Green Mole, 116
    Red Mole Sauce, 124
Mole de jengibre con pechugas de pollo, 129
Monkfish
    Seafood Stew, 109–10
"Mortar" Salsa, 162
Mushrooms
    Beef Tenderloin Filets with Shiitakes in Morita Chile and
        Tomatillo Sauce, 119
    Grilled Portobellos with Chipotle Sauce, 52
    Halibut in Parchment with Tequila, 94
    Mixed-Mushroom Tacos, 64
    Mushroom Sauce, 101
Mussels
    Mussels with White Wine, Serranos, and Cilantro, 111
    Seafood Stew, 109–10

Nieve de tuna con galletas de lima, 184
Nopales
    buying, 25
    Cactus Salad, 89
    Grilled Cactus and Seafood Napoleons with Chipotle
        Cream, 33
Nopales rellenos con mariscos y chipotle, 33

Octopus Salad, Grilled, 82
Oils
    Chile Oil, 139
    Cilantro Oil, 169
Olives
    Lobster Seviche with Oranges and Serranos, 38
    Pork Picadillo Turnovers, 62–63
    Veracruz Tomato Sauce, 102
Onions
    Beet and Onion Strings, 44
    Caramelized Onions, 86
Oranges
    Christmas Eve Salad, 90
    Lobster Seviche with Oranges and Serranos, 38
    Orange-Flavored Flan, 179
    peeling and segmenting, 90
    Pomegranate-Orange Sauce, 135
Ostiones con crema de chipotle, 112
Oysters in Chipotle Cream Sauce, 112

Papas con chorizo, 145
Papas con crema y queso añejo, 146
Papas con espinaca y cebollas, 145
Papaya–Tequila Sauce, Red, 97
Pasteles de chocolate con crema de café, 174
Pastel tres leches, 176
Pato almendrado, 133–34
Pear and Mango Tartlets, 180–81
Peas
    Mexican Rice, 153
Pescado a la veracruzana, 102
Pescado alcaparrado con chilacas rellenas, 105
Pescado al tequila, 94
Pescado con hongos y dos salsas, 101
Pierna de pato con granada, 135–36
Piloncillo, 25
Pineapple
    Ancho-Chile Sauce, 123
    Caramelized Pineapple, 183
    Grilled Portobellos with Chipotle Sauce, 52
    Lentil Soup, 74
    Pineapple Sorbet, 183
    Pineapple Three Ways, 183
    Pineapple "Tuiles," 183
Pine nuts
    buying, 25
    toasting, 26
Plantains
    Ancho-Chile Sauce, 123
    Veal Chops with Black Bean and Habanero Sauce, 120
Poblanos rellenos con papas y aguacate, 55
Pollitos con salsa de guajillo, 130
Pomegranates
    Duck Leg Confit with Pomegranate, 135–36
    Pomegranate-Orange Sauce, 135
    removing seeds from, 136
Pork. *See also* Bacon; Chorizo, Mexican
    Pork Chops with Ancho-Chile Sauce, 123
    Pork Picadillo Turnovers, 62–63

Shredded Pork with Roasted Tomatoes and Chipotle
Chiles, 60
Portobellos enchipotlados a la parilla, 52
Potatoes
Cold Marinated Beef Brisket, 59
Potato Cakes with Aged Mexican Cheese, 146
Potatoes with Chorizo, 145
Potatoes with Spinach and Onions, 145
Scalloped Potatoes, 146
Stuffed Poblano Chiles with Avocado and Potatoes, 55
Prickly pears
preparing, 25
Prickly Pear Sorbet in Lime Tuiles, 184
Pumpkin seeds
Baby Racks of Lamb with a Pumpkin-Seed Crust, 127
Green Mole, 116
toasting, 26
uses for, 26
Puré de chile ancho o guajillo, 165
Purslane Salad, 85

Quail, Grilled, with Ancho-Honey Sauce, 139

Rajas con crema, 142
Red snapper
Fish Fillets Veracruz-Style, 102
Fish in Caper Sauce with Stuffed Chilaca Chiles, 105
Rice
Mexican Rice, 153
Rice Pudding Brûlée, 178
Rice with Poblano Chiles, 150
White Rice, 150

Salad dressings
Chipotle-Honey Dressing, 86
Chipotle Vinaigrette, 59
Lime-Oregano Dressing, 82
Salads
Cactus Salad, 89
Christmas Eve Salad, 90
Grilled Octopus Salad, 82
Purslane Salad, 85
Spinach Salad with Chipotle-Honey Dressing, 86
Salmon
Ancho-Glazed Salmon with Fennel, 98
Salmon with Red Papaya–Tequila Sauce, 97
Tequila-Cured Salmon Tartare with Tuna, 47
Salmón al hinojo glaseado con chile ancho, 98
Salmón con salsa de papaya roja y tequila, 97
Salpicón de carne, 59
Salsa de aguacate y tomatillo, 162
Salsa de chile ancho y miel, 166
Salsa de chile de árbol, 158
Salsa de cuatro chiles, 166
Salsa de jitomate asado y chipotle, 161
Salsa de mango, 171
Salsa de molcajete, 162
Salsa de tomatillo asado, 165

Sauces (*salsas*)
Almond Mole, 133
Ancho-Chile Sauce, 123
Ancho-Honey Sauce, 166
Árbol Chile Sauce, 158
Avocado-Habanero Sauce, 43
Avocado-Tomatillo Sauce, 162
Black Bean and Habanero Sauce, 120
Black Bean Sauce, 51
Chipotle Seafood Sauce, 33
Coffee Bean Sauce, 174
Four-Chile Sauce, 166
Ginger Mole, 129
Grapefruit-Corn Salsa, 97
Green Mole, 116
Green Salsa, 34
Mango Sauce, 171
Morita Chile and Tomatillo Sauce, 119
"Mortar" Salsa, 162
Mushroom Sauce, 101
Pasilla Sauce, 128
Pasilla-Tomatillo Sauce, 127
Pomegranate-Orange Sauce, 135
Red Mole Sauce, 124
Red Papaya–Tequila Sauce, 97
Roasted Poblano Cream Sauce, 169
Roasted Tomatillo Sauce, 165
Roasted Tomato–Chipotle Sauce, 161
Salsa Mexicana, 48
Spicy Chimichurri, 62
Sweet Garlic Sauce, 106
Veracruz Tomato Sauce, 102
wine and, 18
Scallops
Bacon-Wrapped Sea Scallops, 30
Seafood Stew, 109–10
Sea bass
Black Sea Bass with Mushrooms and Two Sauces, 101
Fish in Caper Sauce with Stuffed Chilaca Chiles, 105
Seafood Stew, 109–10
Sesame seeds
buying, 26
Ginger Mole, 129
Green Mole, 116
toasting, 26
Seviche
Fish Seviche, 37
Lobster Seviche with Oranges and Serranos, 38
Seviche de langosta con naranjas y serranos, 38
Seviche de pescado clásico, 37
Shrimp
Chipotle Seafood Sauce, 33
Grilled Cactus and Seafood Napoleons with Chipotle
Cream, 33
Grilled Shrimp with Two Sauces, 41
Seafood Stew, 109–10
Simple Syrup, 171
Sopa de elote y anís, 81

Sopa de lentejas, 74
Sopa fría de aguacate y jaiba, 78
Sorbet
Pineapple Sorbet, 183
Prickly Pear Sorbet in Lime Tuiles, 184
Spicy Cucumber Sorbet, 77
Soups
Chilled Avocado and Crab Soup, 78
Corn Soup with Star Anise, 81
Lentil Soup, 74
Mexican-Style Gazpacho with Spicy Cucumber
Sorbet, 77
Spinach
Ancho-Glazed Salmon with Fennel, 98
Oysters in Chipotle Cream Sauce, 112
Potatoes with Spinach and Onions, 145
Spinach Salad with Chipotle-Honey Dressing, 86
Spinach Tamales, 154
Squash
Squash Blossoms Stuffed with Goat Cheese, 56
Zucchini and Chipotle Tamales, 69
Stock, Fish, 109
Sweet potatoes and yams
Ancho-Chile Sauce, 123
Langoustines with "Raw" Green Salsa, 34
shredding, 34

Tacos, Mixed-Mushroom, 64
Tacos con hongos, 64
Tamales
Black Bean and Chihuahua Cheese Tamales, 68
Cheese and Chile Tamales, 70
Spinach Tamales, 154
tips for, 67
Zucchini and Chipotle Tamales, 69
Tamales de calabaza y chipotle, 69
Tamales de frijoles negros con queso, 68
Tamales de queso fresco y chile serrano, 70
Tamales espinaca, 154
Tartaletas de pera y mango, 180–81
Tártaro de salmón curado al tequila y atún, 47
Tartlets, Pear and Mango, 180–81
Tequila
Halibut in Parchment with Tequila, 94
Lobster Seviche with Oranges and Serranos, 38
Red Papaya–Tequila Sauce, 97
Tequila-Cured Salmon Tartare with Tuna, 47
Tequila Truffles, 175
"Three Milks" Cake, 176
Tinga de puerco, 60
Tomatillos
Avocado-Tomatillo Sauce, 162
Crab Cakes with Avocado-Habanero Sauce, 43–44
Green Mole, 116
Green Salsa, 34
Morita Chile and Tomatillo Sauce, 119
Pasilla-Tomatillo Sauce, 127
peeling, 26
Roasted Tomatillo Sauce, 165

Tomatoes
    Almond Mole, 133
    Árbol Chile Sauce, 158
    Grilled Octopus Salad, 82
    Lentil Soup, 74
    Lobster Seviche with Oranges and Serranos, 38
    Mexican Rice, 153
    Mexican-Style Gazpacho with Spicy Cucumber
        Sorbet, 77
    "Mortar" Salsa, 162
    peeling and seeding, 26
    Pinto Beans with Bacon and Poblano Chiles, 149
    Pork Picadillo Turnovers, 62–63
    Purslane Salad, 85
    Red Mole Sauce, 124
    Roasted Poblano Strips with Cream, 142
    Roasted Tomato–Chipotle Sauce, 161
    roasting, 26
    Salsa Mexicana, 48
    Shredded Pork with Roasted Tomatoes and
        Chipotle Chiles, 60
    storing, 26
    Veracruz Tomato Sauce, 102
Tortas de jaiba con salsa de aguacate y habanero, 43–44
Tortas de papa con queso añejo, 146
Tortillas
    Mixed-Mushroom Tacos, 64
    Tostaditas, 60
Trio de piña, 183
Trufas de tequila, 175
Truffles, Tequila, 175
Tuna, Tequila-Cured Salmon Tartare with, 47

Vanilla Flans, 179
Veal Chops with Black Bean and Habanero Sauce, 120
Veracruz Tomato Sauce, 102

Wine, 17–19

Yams. *See* Sweet potatoes and yams

Zucchini and Chipotle Tamales, 69

table of equivalents

The exact equivalents in the following tables have been rounded for convenience.

LIQUID/DRY MEASURES

U.S.	Metric
¼ teaspoon	1.25 milliliters
½ teaspoon	2.5 milliliters
1 teaspoon	5 milliliters
1 tablespoon (3 teaspoons)	15 milliliters
1 fluid ounce (2 tablespoons)	30 milliliters
¼ cup	60 milliliters
⅓ cup	80 milliliters
½ cup	120 milliliters
1 cup	240 milliliters
1 pint (2 cups)	480 milliliters
1 quart (4 cups, 32 ounces)	960 milliliters
1 gallon (4 quarts)	3.84 liters
1 ounce (by weight)	28 grams
1 pound	454 grams
2.2 pounds	1 kilogram

LENGTH

U.S.	Metric
⅛ inch	3 millimeters
¼ inch	6 millimeters
½ inch	12 millimeters
1 inch	2.5 centimeters

OVEN TEMPERATURE

Fahrenheit	Celsius	Gas
250	120	½
275	140	1
300	150	2
325	160	3
350	180	4
375	190	5
400	200	6
425	220	7
450	230	8
475	240	9
500	260	10